ENGLAND, IRELAND,

AND

AMERICA

ENGLAND, IRELAND,

AND

AMERICA

by
RICHARD COBDEN

with an Introduction by Richard Ned Lebow

A Publication of the
Institute for the Study of Human Issues
Philadelphia

Manufactured in the United States of America

Library of Congress Cataloging in Publication Data:

Cobden, Richard, 1804–1865.
  England, Ireland, and America.

  Originally published in 1835.
  Reprinted from the 1903 ed. of The political writings of Richard Cob-
den published by T. Fisher Unwin, London.
  Includes bibliographical references.
  1. Great Britain—Foreign relations—1800–1837. 2. Ireland—Eco-
nomic conditions. 3. United States—Economic conditions—To 1865.
I. Title.
DA540.C63   1978   327.41   77–28350
ISBN 0–915980–44–4

For information, write:
Director of Publications
ISHI
3401 Science Center
Philadelphia, Pennsylvania 19104
U.S.A.

CONTENTS.

INTRODUCTION
TO THE REPRINT EDITION.

RICHARD NED LEBOW.

As calico printers go, Richard Cobden was an exceptional man. A Manchester manufacturer, parliamentary crusader for free trade and apostle of international cooperation, he became one of the most prominent figures of Victorian Britain. His biographers insist that he was also one of the most misunderstood; that his association in the popular mind with the repeal of the Corn Laws obscured his wider vision of society in which the fight against protection was merely one important step toward a new social order.[1]

Cobden was born into very modest circumstances on June 3, 1804. His father, a Sussex farmer, had difficulties making ends meet and was forced to sell his farm in 1814. The intercession of his uncle, a London merchant, enabled the young Richard to continue his schooling. He was sent to Bowes Hall, a Yorkshire public school, where he lived a life of almost total seclusion for the next five years. He was poorly fed, physically abused and ill-taught and remembered these years as the most miserable of his life. His agony came to an end in 1819 when a kindly usher wrote to his father describing his son's poor health and unhappiness.

Back in London Cobden went to work as a clerk in his uncle's warehouse. After a five-year apprenticeship he was sent on the road with samples of muslin and calico prints. For the next three years he traveled all over England collecting orders. By 1828 he felt sufficiently experienced to leave his uncle's employ and go into business for himself. With two friends in Manchester he began selling dry goods on commission. In 1831, parliament abolished the export excise on calicoes, removing an important impediment to the growth of the Midlands cotton industry. Excited by the prospect of unrestricted export, Cobden and his partners bought an old calico factory at Sabden, twenty-eight miles from Manchester. Their enterprise prospered and by 1836 brought in a profit of £23,000.

Cobden's intellectual development began only after he had left school. During the years of his apprenticeship he read widely, especially in the field of political economy. Adam Smith became his favorite author and he carried *The Wealth of Nations* with him on his travels as many of his contemporaries did the Bible. During the course of these journeys and later ones to Ireland (1825–26), the United States (1835), the Ottoman Empire (1836–37) and the Continent (1846–47), Cobden showed himself to be a shrewd observer. He picked up a wealth of practical information which provided a nice counterpoint to the intellectual notions he imbibed from his readings. He also drew upon this experience in his writings and speeches to provide empirical illustrations and documentation for his arguments, thereby giving them a greater ring of authenticity.

Cobden's interest in politics first became apparent in Sabden, where he gave speeches in favor of making education more widely available to young people. He also wrote a series of anonymous letters to Manchester newspapers in 1835 on the subject of incorporation.[2] Earlier, he had written a political comedy, *The Phrenologist,* which fortunately for Cobden's subsequent reputation was rejected by the manager of the Covent Garden Theater in London.

These hesitant efforts aside, Cobden's first serious attempt to express himself on a question of national importance was his pamphlet, *England, Ireland, and America,* published in the spring of 1835. James Ridgway, the publisher, had told Cobden that nobody should write a pamphlet unless he had some purpose other than mere publication. Cobden confessed to having such a goal "in distant and dim perspective."[3] We can be reasonably certain that he was already contemplating a political career and hoped that the pamphlet would bring his name to the public's attention.

This aspiration was certainly fulfilled. Within a year the pamphlet went through three editions at the relatively high price of 3/6. By April 1836 a cheap edition was selling for 6d. Much of the pamphlet's success was due to the effusive praise it received from the press. The *Manchester Guardian* described Cobden in a lead article as an acute and original thinker, a clear and interesting writer and a man of a liberal and comprehensive mind.[4] *The Times,* not exactly a bastion of liberal thinking, nevertheless declared that the pamphlet had "some sound views of the true foreign policy of England, and some just and forcible reflections on the causes which keep us in the rear of improvement. . . ."[5] Cobden was well on his way toward becoming a figure of national note.

The immediate purpose of the pamphlet was to refute the view that the national interest required protecting Turkey against Russian encroachment. An impassioned appeal to this effect had been made by the former secretary of the British embassy in Constantinople, whose popular pamphlet was part of an ultimately successful effort to create an Anglo-French alliance to check Russian expansion toward the Mediterranean. The Near Eastern question, a highly controversial one at the time, was of no intrinsic interest to Cobden. It nevertheless provided him with an opportunity to advance his unorthodox views about the proper role of foreign policy. The pamphlet is significant in its attempt to illuminate the linkages between foreign and domestic policy, a theme Cobden would hammer away at throughout his career. *England, Ireland, and America* is in many ways a blueprint for that career, since it articulates and develops the basic premises upon which Cobden would predicate his future political activity. Cobden himself recognized this. Years later, in a letter to his friend and mentor George Combe, he referred to the pamphlet as containing "many crude details (which I should not now print), but upon whose three broad propositions I have never changed my opinion. They were—First, that the great curse of our policy has been our love of intervention in foreign politics; secondly, that our greatest home difficulty is Ireland; and thirdly, that the United States is the greatest *economical* rival which will rule the destiny of England."[6]

The organization of the pamphlet reflects these three concerns. The first part, entitled, "England," is an indictment of the notion of the balance of power. In the name of that principle, Cobden asserts, Britain has intervened in quarrels all over Europe. This incessant "meddling" in the affairs of others has proven extremely costly and has in no way advanced British security or trade. A contention like this which repudiated the accepted dogma of the day required careful elaboration if the author had any hope of persuading readers to adopt his point of view. This Cobden did not really provide. He ignored the question of security—surely the most compelling foreign concern to Englishmen of his time—in favor of the trade issue. He attempted to show that wars cannot be fought to protect or expand commerce since trade patterns are largely independent of political relationships. In support of this argument he analyzed the failure of Napoleon's Continental System and the success of Anglo-American trade, the former as a compelling example of how economic interest triumphs over political restraints, the latter as evidence that trade can prosper even after political authority declines.

In subsequent arguments Cobden seemed to imply that the balance of power is more an expression than a cause of conflict. He suggested that the underlying reason for English intervention in Continental affairs was national vanity which encouraged Englishmen to believe that it was their mission to uphold the rights of other nations and the functioning of the international system in general. "In truth, Great Britain has, in contempt of the dictates of prudence and self-interest, an insatiable thirst to become the peace-maker abroad, or if that benevolent task fail her, to assume the office of gensdarme, and keep in order, gratuitously, all the refractory nations of Europe."[7] This charge certainly has a familiar ring to American ears since our own country has so recently been criticized for aspiring to the role of world policeman.

Like many contemporary critics of American foreign policy Cobden advocated strict isolationism as the proper antidote to a ruinous policy of intervention. "Who does not now see," he declared, "that, to have shut ourselves in our own ocean fastness, and to have guarded its shores and its commerce by our fleets, was the line of policy we ought never to have departed from—and who is there that is not now *feeling,* in the burthen of our taxation, the dismal errors of our departure from this rule during the last [Napoleonic] war?" Britain should heed Washington's advice to his countrymen to extend commercial relations with all nations but to have as little political connection with them as possible. That this was Cobden's central theme is attested to by his reproduction of Washington's words to this effect as an epigraph for the pamphlet.

It is important to point out that Cobden's plea for political isolation was motivated by his belief that it was not only advantageous to Britain but to the international community as a whole. It would promote peace by allowing commerce to flourish, for "commerce is the grand panacea, which, like a beneficent medical discovery, will serve to inoculate with the healthy and saving taste for civilisation all the nations of the world." Revealing some of the same national vanity he found so infuriating in his opponents, Cobden went on to declare that "Not a bale of merchandise leaves our shores, but it bears the seeds of intelligence and fruitful thought to the members of some less enlightened community; not a merchant visits our seats of manufacturing industry, but he returns to his own country the missionary of freedom, peace, and good government—whilst our steamboats, that now visit every port of Europe, and our miraculous railroads, that are the talk of all nations, are the advertisements and vouchers for the value of our enlightened institutions." Trade, not the sword, would carry progress around the world. It would bring into being an international community of interest and create such a degree of mutual dependence as to make war an increasingly unthinkable prospect.

Cobden's development and constant reiteration of this theme marks him as the founder of the school of internationalism that has played such a large part in Anglo-American thinking about foreign relations. His disciples and intellectual descendants include John Morley, J. A. Hobson and E. D. Morel in Britain and Woodrow Wilson in the United States. They all subscribed to Cobden's view that war was an inherently irrational policy which appealed only to backward, unrepresentative governments and that once these governments were swept away by the march of progress international disputes could be regulated by arbitration and law.

The second part of the pamphlet is concerned with the state of Ireland, a subject with which the author had some firsthand experience. Ireland, according to Cobden, was a land of "poverty, ignorance, and misrule." It presented "a grosser spectacle of moral and physical debasement" than was to be encountered anywhere else in the civilized world. Cobden found it particularly galling that so much national wealth had been squandered in foreign wars while the welfare of the Irish, for whom England was directly responsible, had largely been ignored.

Cobden ascribed Ireland's backwardness to her lack of commerce, a condition he found something of an anomaly given the country's fertile soil, fine rivers and favored geographic position. This lack of trade he attributed in the first place to centuries of British restrictions which had a disastrous effect upon Irish commercial and industrial development. A further cause of stagnation, he suggested, was the strength of the Catholic religion among the Irish people. The argument he offered in support of this contention is remarkable in the extent to which it presaged Max Weber's *The Protestant Ethic and the Spirit of Capitalism.*

Cobden disavowed any knowledge as to which form of religion might be spiritually superior. He wished to limit his analysis to the effect of different religions upon the secular prosperity of nations. Citing as evidence the prosperity of the Protestant parts of France, Germany and Switzerland in contrast to the relative backwardness of the Catholic regions of these countries, Cobden concluded that there must be something about the Catholic religion that tends to discourage the perseverance, drive and concern for personal betterment that are so essential to commercial development. His analysis of Switzerland was deceptively empirical. Of the twenty-two cantons, Cobden described ten as primarily Catholic, eight as largely Protestant and four as mixed. He found the Catholic cantons to be wholly agricultural, the Protestant ones principally devoted to manufacturing and the mixed cantons giving evidence of both agricultural pursuits and commercial enterprise. The telling point for him was the division to be found within the mixed cantons, where Catholics appeared to engage in farming and Protestants in industry.

The lesson Cobden drew from this exercise is an interesting one. The Catholic religion, he insisted, exercised such a profound influence over the Irish people because it had been persecuted: "persecution . . . has done for this Church what, under the circumstances, nothing besides could have achieved; it has enabled it to resist, not only unscathed, but actually with augmented power, the shocks of a free press, and the liberalising influence of the freest constitutional government in Europe." To reduce the sway of the Church it was necessary to put it on an equal footing with the Protestant religion by ending state support for the latter. Toleration, he believed, would actually promote the cause of the Reformation in Ireland by encouraging the Irish to consider the advantages of the Protestant faith in an atmosphere uncharged with emotion. Cobden's arrogance aside, his suggestion does reveal insight into the role oppression plays in solidifying group identity.

With respect to more immediate palliatives for the Irish problem, Cobden put little faith in most of the nostrums being debated by his contemporaries. He opposed legislation requiring absentee landlords to reside in Ireland as unenforceable. He described the introduction of a poor law as equally impractical because nobody could afford the rates that would be required to support the large number of indigent persons. Repeal of the Act of Union with Britain, the preferred remedy of the Irish themselves, he dismissed as irrelevant and certain to lead to the creation of a corrupt and unresponsive parliament in Dublin. Cobden favored modest emigration combined with some program of economic development as the only practical solution to Ireland's woes. As an important first step toward economic progress, he advocated the development of a harbor on the west coast to serve as a major port and trans-shipment point for the growing transatlantic trade.

In later years Cobden became much less optimistic about the prospect of transforming Ireland even though he continued to believe that it was England's most pressing problem. The Repeal agitation of the 1840s, which actually intensified during the famine, convinced him that Irish M.P.s had little real interest in improving their country. Cobden became extremely intolerant of their views and even suggested that some of the Irish leaders belonged in a lunatic asylum.[8] Like many other Englishmen Cobden succumbed to the temptation of explaining the depressed state of Ireland in terms of the degenerate character of her people. "The real difficulty in Ireland," he wrote to George Combe in October 1848, "is the character and condition socially and morally of the people, from the peer to the Connaught peasant. It is not by forms of legislation or the locality of parliaments, but by a change and improvement of the population, that Ireland is to have a start in the career of civilization and self-government."[9] Cobden also expressed frustration at the power of the landlords, both English and Irish, who blocked any attempt to reform the system of land tenure in Ireland. He saw little chance that their influence could be overcome short of a radical revision of the electoral franchise.[10]

The final part of the pamphlet describes the striking economic development of the United States which Cobden believed would one day lead to its commercial ascendancy over

Britain. Perhaps the most novel aspect of this section is the wealth of statistical evidence Cobden adduced in support of his contention. His attention was drawn not only to trade and production figures but also to the present state and projected growth of population, transportation (i.e., railways and canals), schools per capita, newspapers and capital. Contemporary social scientists consider these to be among the more reliable indices of modernization and Cobden's use of them for the same purpose reveals remarkable insight on his part into the nature of industrial development.

Cobden's real purpose in documenting the growing economic power of America was to prove the utility of the political and economic policies he advocated for his own country by demonstrating that they had been responsible for American prosperity. America's primary advantage over England, Cobden insisted, was her policy of isolation which required her to maintain only a small military establishment, thereby permitting her to expend resources in more productive ways. In contrast, Cobden found that Britain allocated over £13 million a year for defense, an expenditure he believed to constitute a serious drain on the wealth of the country. The same argument has been made in our own day to help explain the phenomenal growth of postwar Germany and Japan. As formulated by Cobden, it ignored some of the positive effects defense spending may have had upon economic growth. However, Cobden must be given high marks for his assertion that colonies, a major justification for a large fleet, ultimately result in considerable pecuniary loss to the mother country. It is tantalizing that he left the development of this thesis to "some abler pen" in light of the prevalence until recent times of the opposite view.

Cobden urged Englishmen to emulate the example of America by practicing economy at home, nonintervention abroad, and by introducing a number of public improvements, among them universal education, that would encourage greater prosperity. He favored cutting the defense and foreign office budgets by fully 50 percent in order to ensure that Europe would be left to stew in her own quarrels. His final recommendation was for repeal of the Corn Laws, a legislative action for which Cobden would shortly lead a crusade and with which his name would forever be associated. He believed that the free importation of grain would act as a tremendous stimulus to British industry by providing grain-exporting countries with credits with which to purchase British goods. It would also lower the cost of those manufactures by making cheap bread available to the laboring classes.

From the vantage point of the late twentieth century this pamphlet, indeed Cobden's entire philosophy, appears somewhat naive and morally arrogant. But it is also refreshing. Cobden's buoyant optimism, his certainty of the links between morality and action and his belief that a secular millenium lay around the corner bespeak a faith in mankind that is unacceptable to our wary and disillusioned intellects. Cobden's belief in the perfectability of man was even a bit extreme for most of his Victorian contemporaries, some of whom described him as too much under the influence of Continental, especially French philosophy.[11] But Cobden's philosophy of civilization was really a direct expression of his personal experiences in the Midlands. He spent his most formative years in the very cockpit of the industrial revolution and was struck by the incredible human energy the manufacturing process had released and the manner in which it had already begun to transform society. He believed that this energy, an expression of enlightened self-interest, was a tremendous positive force that would bring about an international community of interest transcending the artificial antagonisms of class, nationality, religion and race. But first it was necessary to remove the fetters of both law and custom that restricted the free exchange of goods and ideas.

Cobden's underlying purpose in writing *England, Ireland, and America* was to make his countrymen aware of these barriers to progress. It is this theme that binds together the three otherwise disparate sections of the pamphlet. Each was intended to illustrate how the pernicious influence of the aristocracy, exercised through that class's control of parliament, was the great obstacle to all improvement. In Ireland, the landed gentry blocked land reform and disestablishment, urgently required to ameliorate the condition of the country, because rack renting and the tithe provided a major source of their income. In England, they upheld protection, despite its retrograde effect upon the economy, because it artificially inflated the profits of their estates. Most damaging of all, they compelled the nation to pursue a policy of colonial expansion and intervention which provided their justification as a class. "The battle-plain," Cobden declared, "is the harvest-field of the aristocracy, watered with the blood of the people." The interests of the middle and working classes were to be preserved by peace. This and other common interests like free trade could be achieved only by limiting the powers of government and the aristocracy.

It seems peculiar to us that anybody would suggest the curtailment of already limited governmental power as a means of achieving social justice. Even Americans have come to accept governmental intervention as the only means of ameliorating the worst effects of many economic and social diseases. Cobden's advocacy of laissez-faire was rooted in a profound conviction that enlightened self-interest, untrammeled by restrictions, was the true instrument of progress and harmony. Our view is that progress depends upon the regulation and restraint of self-interest in order to promote the social good. Neither formulation has achieved the goals its proponents expected it would.

NOTES

1. John Morley, *The Life of Richard Cobden* (London, 1883) and J. A. Hobson, *Richard Cobden: The International Man* (New York, 1919). Hobson makes this point in the very first paragraph of his preface.

2. Morley, pp. 15–17.

3. *Ibid.,* p. 27.

4. *Manchester Guardian,* May 23, 1835.

5. *The Times,* May 5, 1836.

6. Richard Cobden to George Combe, October 4, 1848. This letter is reprinted in Morley, pp. 314–16.

7. Unless otherwise noted, all further quotations are from *England, Ireland, and America.* The edition reprinted in this volume was originally published by T. Fisher Unwin of London in 1903, in the first volume of *The Political Writings of Richard Cobden.*

8. Richard Cobden to H. Ashworth, July 21, 1848. Reprinted in Morley, p. 313.

9. Letter cited in note 6.

10. For Cobden's views on the land question see his letter to George Combe, already cited, and Chapter Nine of Donald Read, *Cobden and Bright: A Victorian Political Partnership* (New York, 1968).

11. Both Morley, p. 94, and Hobson, p. 19, refer to Cobden's "French" spirit.

ENGLAND, IRELAND, AND AMERICA.

1835.

" The great rule of conduct for us in regard to foreign nations is, in extending our commercial relations, to have with them as little *political* connection as possible."—*Washington's farewell address to the American people.*

Part I

ENGLAND.

To maintain what is denominated the true balance of European power has been the fruitful source of wars from the earliest time; and it would be instructive, if the proposed limits of this work permitted it, to bring into review all the opposite struggles into which England has plunged for the purpose of adjusting, from time to time, according to the ever-varying theories of her rulers, this national equilibrium. Let it suffice to say, that history exhibits us, at different periods, in the act of casting our sword into the scale of every European State. In the meantime, events have proclaimed, but in vain, how futile must be our attempts to usurp the sceptre of the Fates. Empires have arisen unbidden by us; others have departed, despite our utmost efforts to preserve them. All have undergone a change so complete that, were the writers who only a century ago lauded the then existing state of the balance of Europe to reappear, they would be startled to find, in the present relations of the Continent, no vestige of that perfect adjustment which had been purchased at the price of so much blood. And yet we have able writers and statesmen of the present day, who would advocate a war to prevent a derangement of what we now choose to pronounce the just equipoise of the power of Europe.

For a period of six hundred years, the French and English people had never ceased to regard each other as natural enemies. Scarcely a generation passed over its allotted section of this vast interval of time without sacrificing its victims to the spirit of national hate. It was reserved for our own day to witness the close of a feud, the bloodiest, the longest, and yet, in its consequences, the most nugatory of any that is to be found in the annals of the world. Scarcely had we time to indulge the first emotions of pity and amazement at the folly of past ages, when, as if to justify to the letter the sarcasm of Hume, when alluding to another subject,* we, the English people, are preparing, through the vehicles of opinion, the public press, to enter upon a hostile career with Russia.

Russia, and no longer France, is the chimera that now haunts us in our apprehension for the safety of Europe : whilst Turkey, for the first time, appears to claim our sympathy and protection against the encroachments of her neighbours ; and, strange as it may appear to the politicians of a future age, such is the prevailing sentiment of hostility towards the Russian government at this time in the public mind, that, with but few additional provocatives administered to it by a judicious minister through the public prints, a conflict with that Christian power, in defence of a Mahomedan people, more than a thousand miles distant from our shores, might be made palatable, nay, popular, with the British nation. It would not be difficult to find a cause for this antipathy : the impulse, as usual with large masses of human beings, is a generous one, and arises, in great part, from emotions of pity for the gallant Polish people, and of indigna-tion at the conduct of their oppressors—sentiments in which we cordially and zealously concur : and if it were the province of Great Britain to administer justice to all the people of the earth—in other words, if God had given us, as a nation, the authority and the power, together with the wisdom and the goodness, sufficient to qualify us to deal forth His vengeance— then should we be called upon in this case to rescue the weak from the hands of their spoilers. But do we possess these

---

* "Though in a future age it will probably become difficult to persuade some nations that any human two-legged creature could ever embrace such principles. And it is a thousand to one but those nations themselves shall have something fully as absurd in their own creed, to which they will give a most implicit consent."

favoured endowments? Are we armed with the powers of Om-
nipotence : or, on the contrary, can we discover another people
rising into strength with a rapidity that threatens inevitably to
overshadow us? Again, do we find ourselves to possess the
virtue and the wisdom essential to the possession of supreme
power; or, on the other hand, have we not at our side, in the
wrongs of a portion of our own people, a proof that we can
justly lay claim to neither?

Ireland and the United States of America ought to be the
subjects of our inquiry at this period, when we are, apparently,
preparing ourselves to engage as parties to a question involving
countries with which we are but remotely, and in comparison,
very little interested. Before entering upon some reflections
under each of these heads, we shall call the consideration of
our readers to the affairs of Russia and Turkey ; and we shall use
as the text of our remarks a pamphlet that has recently made
its appearance under the title of "England, France, Russia,
and Turkey," to which our attention was first attracted by the
favourable comments bestowed upon it by the influential portion
of the daily press.

The writer * appears to be versed in the diplomatic mysteries
of the courts of St. Petersburg and Constantinople : indeed,
he hints that he has been himself a party to the negotiations
carried on with the Sublime Porte. He says, p. 77—" The
details into which we have already entered may probably
contain internal evidence of our opinion not having been
formed in a closet, remote from the subject we are treating."
And the concluding words of the pamphlet are calculated to
lead to a similar inference ; and they are, moreover, curious,
as illustrating the tone of feeling with which the author regards
the Russian government :—" Our words have been fewer than
our thoughts ; and, while we have to regret abler hands have
not wielded our arms, we owe it to our subject to state, that

* [Mr. Urquhart, formerly Secretary of the English Embassy at Constantinople.]

others, unproduced, prudence forbade to draw until the *hour of retribution arrives.*"

After a preliminary appeal to the sympathies of his readers in favour of Poland, he proceeds to ask, " Is the substance of Turkey to be added to the growth of Russia ? Is the mammoth of the Sarmatian plains to become the leviathan of the Hesperian seas ? Is another victim to be sacrificed within so short a time on the same altar, and because the same trifling succour is again withheld ? Are the remains of Turkey to be laid upon the tomb of Poland, to exclude every ray of hope, and render its doom irrevocable ? "

To what extent this trifling succour is meant to go will be explained in the writer's own words by-and-by. But we propose, in this place, to inquire what are the motives that England can have to desire to preserve the Ottoman Empire at the risk of a war, however trifling ? In entering on this question we shall, of course, premise, that no government has the right to plunge its people into hostilities, except in defence of their own national honour or interests. Unless this principle be made the rule of all, there can be no guarantee for the peace of any one country, so long as there may be found a people, whose grievances may attract the sympathy or invite the interference of another State. How, then, do we find our honour or interests concerned in defending the Turkish territory against the encroachments of its Christian neighbour ? It is not alleged that we have an alliance with the Ottoman Porte, which binds us to preserve its empire intact ; nor does there exist, with regard to this country, a treaty between Russia and Great Britain (as was the case with respect to Poland) by which we became jointly guarantees for its separate national existence. The writer we are quoting puts the motive for our interference in a singular point of view ; he says, " This obligation is imposed upon us as members of the European community by the approaching annihilation of another of our compeers. It is imposed upon us by the necessity of maintaining the consideration due to ourselves—the first element of political power and influence." From this it would appear to be the opinion of our author, that our being one of the nations of Europe imposes on us, besides the defence of our own territory, the task of upholding the rights and perpetuating the existence of all the other powers of the Continent, a sentiment common, we fear, to a very large portion of the English public. In truth, Great Britain has, in contempt of the dictates of prudence and self-interest, an insatiable thirst to become the peace-maker abroad, or if that benevolent task fail her, to assume the office of gensdarme, and keep in order, gratuitously, all the refractory nations of Europe. Hence does it arise, that, with an invulnerable island for our territory, more secure against foreign molestation than is any part of the coast of North America, we magnanimously disdain to avail ourselves of the privileges which nature offers to us, but cross the ocean, in quest of quadripartite treaties or quintuple alliances, and, probably, to leave our own good name in pledge for the debts of the poorer members of such confederacies. To the same spirit of overweening national importance may in great part be traced the ruinous wars, and yet more ruinous subsidies, of our past history. Who does not now see that, to have shut ourselves in our own ocean fastness, and to have guarded its shores and its commerce by our fleets, was the line of policy we ought never to have departed from—and who is there that is not now *feeling*, in the burthen of our taxation, the dismal errors of our departure from this rule during the last war? How little wisdom we have gathered along with these bitter fruits of experience, let the subject of our present inquiry determine !

Judging from another passage in this pamphlet, it would appear that England and France are now to be the sole dictators of the international relations of all Europe. The following passage is dictated by that pure spirit of English vanity which has already proved so expensive an appendage to our character; and which, unless allayed by increased knowledge among the people, or fairly crushed out of us by our financial burthens, will, we fear, carry us still deeper into the vortex of debt :—" The squadrons of England and France anchored in the Bosphorus, they dictate their own terms to Turkey ; to Russia they proclaim, that from that day they intend to arbitrate supremely between the nations of the earth."

We know of but one way in which the honour of this country may be involved in the defence and preservation of the Turkish empire ; and that is, through the indiscreet meddling in the intrigues of the seraglio, on the part of our diplomatists. After a few flourishes of the pen, in the style and spirit of the above quotations, shall have passed between the gentlemen of the rival embassies of St. James's and St. Petersburg, who knows but the English nation may, some day, be surprised by the discovery that it is compromised in a quarrel from which there is no honourable escape but by the disastrous course of a long and ruinous war.

If our honour be not committed in this case, still less shall we find, by examining a little more at length, that our *interests* are involved in the preservation of Turkey. To quote again from the pamphlet before us :—" Suffice it to say, that the countries consuming to the yearly value of thirty millions* of our exports, would be placed under the immediate control of the coalition (Russia, Prussia, and Austria), and, of course, under the regulations of the Russian tariff ; not as it is to-day, but such as it would be when the mask is wholly dropped. What would be the effect on the internal state of England, if a considerable diminution of exportation occurred ?   But it is not only the direct effects of the tariffs of the coalition that are to be apprehended : would it not command the tariffs of Northern and Southern America ?"   Passing over, as too chimerical for comment, the allusion to the New World, we here have the argument which has, immediately or remotely, decided us to undertake almost every war in which Great Britain has been

* Official value.

involved—viz., *the defence of our commerce.* And yet it has, over and over again, been proved to the world, that violence and force can never prevail against the natural wants and wishes of mankind : in other words, that despotic laws against freedom of trade never can be executed. " Trade cannot, will not, be forced ; let other nations prohibit by what severity they please, interest will prevail : they may embarrass their own trade, but cannot hurt a nation whose trade is free, so much as themselves." So said a writer* a century ago, whilst experience down to our own day has done nothing but confirm the truth of his maxims ; and yet people would frighten us into war, to prevent the forcible annihilation of our trade ! Can any proofs be offered how visionary are such fears, more conclusive than are to be found in the history of Napoleon's celebrated war against English commerce ? Let us briefly state a few par-ticulars of this famous struggle. The subject, though familiar to everybody, is one the moral of which cannot be too frequently enforced.

The British Islands were, in 1807, declared by Bonaparte in a state of blockade, by those decrees which aimed at the total destruction of the trade of Great Britain. The Berlin and Milan edicts declared—

1. The British Isles were in a state of blockade. 2. All commerce and correspondence were forbidden. All English letters were to be seized in the post-houses. 3. Every English-man, of whatever rank or quality, found in France, or the countries allied with her, was declared a prisoner of war. 4. All merchandise or property, of whatever kind, belonging to English subjects, was declared lawful prize. 5. All articles of English manufacture, and articles produced in her colonies, were, in like manner, declared contraband, and lawful prize.

France, Russia, Austria, Prussia, Holland, Italy, and the States of Germany, joined in this conspiracy against the com-merce of England. To enforce more effectually these prohibi-

* Sir Matthew Decker.

tions, commissioners of rank were appointed to each of the principal seaports of the Continent. Now, let us mark well the result of this great confederation, which was formed for the avowed purpose of annihilating us as a trading people. The following is an account of the declared value of our exports of British products for each of the years mentioned, ending 5th of January :—

1804	.	.	.	.	.	.	£36,100,000
1805	.	.	.	.	.	.	37,100,000
1806	.	.	.	.	.	.	37,200,000
1807	.	.	.	.	.	.	39,700,000
1808	.	.	.	.	.	.	36,400,000
1809	.	.	.	.	.	.	36,300,000

It must be borne in mind that the proclamation of war against our trade, above-mentioned, was dated in 1807. It appears, then, by the preceding tabular view, that our commerce sustained a loss to the extent of about $7\frac{1}{2}$ per cent. in 1808 and 1809, as compared with 1806 and 1807 ; whilst the amount of exports in the year 1808, or 1809, if compared with the mean or average amount of the above six years, shows a diminution only of about two per cent. And all this took place, be it remembered, when two-thirds of our foreign trade was confined to Europe.*

It is singular to observe that, by the following table, the declared value of our exports, during the last six years, has remained nearly stationary, at a point varying from the average of the former series of years only by a fraction.

* It would be amusing, and full of romantic interest, to detail some of the ten thousand justifiable arts invented to thwart this unnatural coalition, which, of necessity, converted almost every citizen of Europe into a smuggler. Bourrienne, who was himself one of the commissioners at Hamburgh, gives some interesting anecdotes in his " Memoirs " under this head. The writer is acquainted with a merchant who was interested in a house that employed five hundred horses in transporting British goods, many of which were landed in Sclavonia, and thence conveyed overland to France, at a charge of about £28 a cwt.—more than fifty times the present freight of merchandise from London to Calcutta !

Below is a table of the exports of the products of British industry for six years, ending 1833 :—

1828	.	.	.	.	.	. £36,400,000
1829	.	.	.	.	.	. 36,200,000
1830	.	.	.	.	.	. 35,200,000
1831	.	.	.	.	.	. 37,700,000
1832	.	.	.	.	.	. 36,600,000
1833	.	.	.	.	.	. 36,000,000

But it must be borne in view, that, as the price of the raw materials of manufactures, such as wool, cotton, silk, iron, &c., together with the price of grain, has undergone a vast depreciation since the former periods, of course the actual exchangeable value of the money amounts in the second table is very much greater than in the first.

In fact, the official value of our exports appears to have doubled, whilst the real or declared value has remained stationary. Bearing all this in mind, still, if we take into consideration the great increase of our exports, since 1809, to the Americas, and to Asia—the quarters where our commerce has been principally increasing—and if we also recollect the higher rate of profits at the earlier periods, it becomes a question if our trade with Europe, notwithstanding its rapid increase in population and wealth, has been benefited by the peace. It is exceedingly doubtful whether, whilst we were engaged in a war for the avowed emancipation of our commerce, our merchants were not, all the while, carrying on a more gainful traffic with the Continent than they now do, when its people have become our bloodless rivals at the loom and the spinning frame.

Where, then, is the wisdom of our fighting European battles in defence of a commerce which knows so well of itself how to elude all its assailants? And what have we to show as a per-contra for the four hundred millions of debt incurred in our last continental wars?

We have dwelt at greater length upon this point, because

the advocates of an intermeddling policy always hold up the alluring prospect of benefiting commerce ; and we think we have said enough to prove that Russian violence cannot destroy, or even sensibly injure, our trade.

But it here becomes proper to ask, Are we warranted in the presumption that Russia is less inclined than other nations for trading with us ?   Our author, indeed, says, p. 90, " Is it for England to allow an empire, a principle of whose existence is freedom of commerce, to be swallowed up by the most restrictive power on the face of the earth ?   Is it for England to allow the first commercial position in the world to be occupied by such a power ?   Is it for England to allow free-dom of commerce to be extinguished in the only portion of Europe where it exists ? "

We are at a loss to account for the ignorance that exists with reference to the comparative importance of our trade with Russia and with Turkey.   The following tables exhibit the amounts of our exports to each of the two countries, at the dates mentioned :—

EXPORTS TO RUSSIA.		EXPORTS TO TURKEY.	
A.D.	£	A.D.	£
1700 .	60,000	1700 .	220,000
1750 .	100,000	1750 .	135,000
1790 .	400,000	1790 .	120,000
1800 .	1,300,000	1800 .	165,000
1820 .	2,300,000	1820 .	800,000*

By which it will be seen that, whilst Turkey has, in more than a century, quadrupled the amount of her purchases, Russia has, in the same interval of time, increased her con-sumption of our goods nearly forty-fold.   Our exports since the year 1700 have increased in a more rapid ratio to Russia than to any other country in Europe.

The rise of the commerce of St. Petersburg is unparal-leled by anything we meet with in Europe, out of England.

* M'Culloch's Dict., 2nd Edit., p. 671.

This city was founded in 1703; in 1714 only sixteen ships entered the port, whilst in 1833 twelve hundred and thirty-eight vessels arrived, and of which no less a proportion than six hundred and ninety-four were British.

Nor must it be forgotten, in drawing a comparison between the value of our trade with Russia and that with Turkey, that, whilst the former has, until very recently, possessed but little sea-coast, with but one good port, and that closed by ice one half of the year, the latter had, down to the date at which we have purposely brought the comparison (when the Greek Islands still formed a portion of the Turkish empire), more than double the extent of maritime territory of any power in Europe, situated in latitudes, too, the most favourable for commerce, including not only the best harbours in the world, but the largest river in Europe.

Neither must it be forgotten that the natural products of the Russian empire are restricted to corn, hemp, tallow, timber, and hides, with a few minor commodities; and that of these, the two important articles of corn and timber are subjected to restrictive, or we might almost say, prohibitive, duties at our hands; whilst Turkey contains the soil and climate adapted for producing almost every article of commerce, with the exception probably only of sugar and tea. We need only mention corn, timber, cotton-wool, sheep's-wool, wood and drugs for dyeing, wine and spirits, tobacco, silk, tallow, hides and skins, coffee, spices, and bullion—to exhibit the natural fertility of a country which is now rendered sterile by the brutalising rule of Mahomedanism. Nor can it be said that commerce is wholly free in Turkey, since the exportation of silk is burthened with a duty, and it is prohibited to export grain,* or any other article of necessity, including the product of the mines.

It is true that this otherwise barbarous government has set an example to more civilised countries, by its

* [This prohibition does not now exist.]

moderate import duties on foreign productions ; and this, we suspect, is the secret of that surprising tenacity of life which exists in the Ottoman empire, notwithstanding the thousand organic diseases that are consuming its body politic.   But what avails to throw open the ports of a country to our ships, if the population will not labour to obtain the produce where-with to purchase our commodities ?

Plains, which Dr. Clarke compares to the fairest portions of Kent, capable of yielding the best silk and cotton, abound in Syria ; but despotic violence has triumphed even over nature ; and this province, which once boasted of Damascus and Antioch, of Tyre, Sidon, and Aleppo, has, by the oppressive exactions of successive pachas, become little better than a de-serted waste.

"Everywhere," says Volney, speaking of Asiatic Turkey, "everywhere I saw only tyranny and misery, robbery and de-vastation.   I found daily on my route abandoned fields, deserted villages, cities in ruins.   Frequently I discovered antique monuments, remains of temples, of palaces, and of fortresses ; pillars, aqueducts, and tombs.   This spectacle led my mind to meditate on past times, and excited in my heart profound and serious thought.   I recalled those ancient ages when twenty famous nations existed in these countries ; I painted to myself the Assyrian on the banks of the Tigris, the Chaldean on those of the Euphrates, the Persian reigning from the Indus to the Mediterranean.   I numbered the kingdoms of Damascus and Idumea, of Jerusalem and Samaria, the war-like States of the Philistines, and the commercial republics of Phœnicia.   This Syria, said I, now almost unpeopled, could then count a hundred powerful cities ; its fields were covered with towns, villages, and hamlets.   Everywhere appeared culti-vated fields, frequented roads, crowded habitations.   What, alas ! has become of those ages of abundance and of life ? What of so many brilliant creations of the hand of man ?   Where are the ramparts of Nineveh, the walls of Babylon, the palaces

of Persepolis, the temples of Baalbec and Jerusalem ? Where
are the fleets of Tyre, the docks of Arad, the looms of Sidon,
and that multitude of sailors, of pilots, of merchants, of
soldiers ? Where are those labourers, those harvests, those
flocks, and that crowd of living beings that then covered the
face of the earth ? Alas ! I have surveyed this ravaged land—
I have visited the places which were the theatre of so much
splendour — and have seen only solitude and desertion.
The temples are crumbled down ; the palaces are over-
thrown ; the ports are filled up ; the cities are destroyed ;
the earth, stripped of its inhabitants, is only a desolate place
of tombs."

No less hideous is the picture given to us by another elo-
quent eye-witness of the desolation of this once flourishing
region.

" A few paltry shops expose nothing but wretchedness to
view, and even these are frequently shut, from apprehension of
the passage of a Cadi.

" Not a creature is to be seen in the streets, not a creature
at the gates, except now and then a peasant gliding through
the gloom, concealing under his garments the fruits of his
labour, lest he should be robbed of his hard earnings by the
rapacious soldier. The only noise heard from time to time is
the galloping of the steed of the desert ; it is the janissary,
who brings the head of the Bedouin, or returns from plundering
the unhappy fellah." *

A still more recent traveller, and one of our own countrymen, has these emphatic words, when speaking of the Turkish
territory : " Wherever the Osmanli has trod devastation and
ruin mark his steps, civilisation and the arts have fled, and
made room for barbarism and the silence of the desert and
the tomb." †

But why need we seek for foreign testimony of the withering and destroying influences of Mahomedanism ? The Turks

* Chateaubriand.   † Macfarlane's Turkey.

themselves have a proverb, which says, " Where the sultan's horse has trod, there no grass grows."

> " And where the Spahi's hoof hath trod,
> The verdure flies the bloody sod."
>
> BYRON.

Our limits do not allow us to dwell on this portion of our task; suffice it to say, that, beneath the sway of Ottoman violence, the pursuits of agriculture and commerce are equally neglected, in regions that once comprised the mart and granary of the world. *No ship was ever seen to leave a Turkish port, manned with Turkish sailors, upon the peaceful errand of foreign mercantile traffic.* On the ocean, as upon land, this fierce people have always been the scourge of humanity, and a barrier to the progress of commerce and civilisation. In their hands, Smyrna, which was termed by the ancients the ornament of Asia, and Constantinople, chosen for the unrivalled seat of empire by one who possessed the sovereignty of the world— these two cities, adapted by nature to become the centres of a vast trade, are now, through the barbarism and indolence of their rulers, little better than nurseries of the plague !

What shall we say more to prove that England can have no interest in perpetuating the commercial bondage of such a land as we have been describing?

Before quitting the consideration of this part of our subject, we will, for a moment, give way to our imagination, and picture the results that would follow, supposing that the population of the United States of America could be moved from their present position on the earth's surface, and in a moment be substituted in the place of the inhabitants of Turkey. Very little difference of latitude opposes itself to the further supposition that the several pachalics, being transformed into free states, should be populated by the natives of such districts of the New World as gave the fittest adaptation to their previous habits of labour. Now, let us picture this empire, after it had been for fifty years only subject to the laws, the religion, and the industry of such a people.

Constantinople, outrivalling New York, may be painted, with a million of free citizens, as the focus of all the trade of eastern Europe. Let us conjure up the thousands of miles of railroads, carrying to the very extremities of this empire—not the sanguinary satrap, but—the merchandise and the busy traders of a free state ; conveying—not the firman of a ferocious sultan, armed with death to the trembling slave, but—the millions of newspapers and letters, which stimulate the enterprise and excite the patriotism of an enlightened people. Let us imagine the Bosphorus and the Sea of Marmora swarming with steamboats, connecting the European and Asiatic continents by hourly departures and arrivals ; or issuing from the Dardanelles, to reanimate once more with life and fertility the hundred islands of the Archipelago ; or, conceive the rich shores of the Black Sea in the power of the New Englander, and the Danube pouring down its produce from the plains of Moldavia and Wallachia, now subject to the plough of the hardy Kentuckian. Let us picture the Carolinians, the Virginians, and the Georgians, transplanted to the coasts of Asia Minor, and behold its hundreds of cities again bursting from the tomb of ages, to recall religion and civilisation to the spot from whence they first issued forth upon the world. Alas ! that this should be only an illusion of the fancy !

There remains another argument in favour of an interposition on our part in defence of Turkey for us to notice ; and it points to the danger our colonies might be in, from any movements which Russia should make eastward. "Our Indian possessions," says the pamphlet before quoted : " shall we fight for them on the Dnieper, as directing the whole Mussulman nation, or shall we fight for them on the Indus, at Bagdad, or in Persia, single-handed ; close to the insurrection she will raise in her rear, and when she is in possession of Turkey ? "

We might have passed over this point as too chimerical for

comment, were it not that it involves a question upon which, we believe, there is greater misapprehension than upon any other subject that engages the attention of our countrymen. Supposing Russia or Austria to be in possession of the Turkish dominions, would she not find her attention and resources far too abundantly occupied in *retaining* the sovereignty over fifteen millions of fierce and turbulent subjects, animated with warlike hatred to their conquerors, and goaded into rebellion by the all-powerful impulse of a haughty and intolerant religion, to contemplate adding still further to her embarrassments by declaring war with England, and giving the word of march to Hindostan ?   Who does not perceive that it could not, for ages at least, add to the *external power* of either of these states, if she were to get possession of Turkey by force of arms ?   Is Russia stronger abroad by her recent perfidious incorporation of Polish territory ?   Would Holland increase her power if she were to reconquer her Belgic provinces to-morrow ?   Or, to come to our own doors, for example, was Great Britain more powerful whilst, for centuries, she held Ireland in disaffected subjection to her rule ; or was she not rather weakened, by offering, in the sister island, a vulnerable point of attack to her continental enemies ?

But supposing, merely by way of argument, that Russia meditated hostile views towards our eastern colonies.

Constantinople is about three thousand miles distant from Calcutta : are our Indian possessions of such value to the British people that we must guard them with operations so extended and so costly as would be necessary if the shores of the Bosphorus are to be made the outpost for our armies or the Ganges ?   Surely it becomes a momentous question, to the already over-burdened people of England, to ascertain what advantages are to be reaped from enterprises like this, which, whatever other results they may chance to involve, are certain to entail increased taxation on themselves.

Nothing, we believe, presents so fair a field for economical analysis, even in this age of new lights, as the subject of colonisation. We can, of course, only briefly allude to the question ; but, in doing so, we suggest it as one that claims the investigation of independent public writers, and of all those members of the legislature who are of and for the people, distinct from selfish views or aristocratic tendencies.

Spain lies, at this moment, a miserable spectacle of a nation whose own natural greatness has been immolated on the shrine of Trans-Atlantic ambition. May not some future historian possibly be found recording a similar epitaph on the tomb of Britain ?

In truth, we have been planting, and supporting, and governing countries upon all degrees of habitable, and some that are not habitable, latitudes of the earth's surface ; and so grateful to our national pride has been the spectacle, that we have never, for once, paused to inquire if our interests were advanced by so much nominal greatness. Three hundred millions of permanent debt have been accumulated—millions of direct taxation are annually levied—restrictions and pro- hibitions are imposed upon our trade in all quarters of the world, for the acquisition or maintenance of colonial pos- sessions ; and all for what ? That we may repeat the fatal Spanish proverb—" The sun never sets on the King of England's dominions." For we believe that no candid investigator of our colonial policy will draw the conclusion that we have derived, or shall derive, from it advantages that can compensate for these formidable sacrifices.

But we are upon the verge of a novel combination of com- mercial *necessities* that will altogether change the relations in which we have hitherto stood with our colonies. We call them necessities, because they will be forced upon us, not from con- viction of the wisdom of such changes, but by the irresistible march of events. The New World is destined to become the arbiter of the commercial policy of the Old. We will see in what manner this is in operation.

At the passing of the Negro Emancipation Act, an effort was made by the merchants of Liverpool, trading to South America, to prevail on the Legislature to abolish the discriminating duties on West India sugar, which operated so severely on the trade with the Brazils.   It was finally decided that the bounty in favour of the importation of our colonial productions should be continued for ten years.   At the end of this period, *if not long before,* therefore, the monstrous impolicy of sacrificing our trade with a new continent, of almost boundless extent of rich territory, in favour of a few small islands, with comparatively exhausted soils, will cease to be sanctioned by the law.   What will then follow?   If we no longer offer the exclusive privileges of our market to the West Indians, we shall cease, as a matter of justice and necessity, to compel them to purchase exclusively from us.   They will be at liberty, in short, to buy wherever they can buy goods cheapest, and to sell in the dearest market.   They must be placed in the very same predicament as if they were not a part of his Majesty's dominions. Where, then, will be the semblance of a plea for putting ourselves to the expense of governing and defending such countries? Let us apply the same test to our other colonies.

It is no longer a debateable question, amongst enlightened and disinterested minds, that the privileges which we give to the Canadian exporters of timber to Britain, and by which alone we command a monopoly of that market for our manufactures, are founded on gross injustice to the people of this country, and are calculated to give a forced misdirection, as all such bounties are, to the natural industry of these colonies, by causing the investment of capital in the preparing and shipping of inferior timber, which would otherwise seek its legitimate employment in the pursuit of agriculture.   This monopoly must yield to the claims of the United States and Baltic trades.   Nor have we been contented with sacrificing our own interests to the promotion of a fictitious prosperity in our colonies, but we destroy the interests of one of these, in the vain hope of benefiting another. Thus, in the same spirit of withering protection, we have awarded to the West Indies a monopoly of the trade to Canada, whilst, to the latter, we give the privilege of exclusively supplying the former with corn and timber: * and all this whilst, at the same time, these islands lie within half the distance of the shores of the United States, whose maritime districts possess all the identical exchangeable products with Canada, and teem with a population of industrious and enterprising people, eager for a commerce with these prohibited people.

True, the Government of the United States has lately compelled us, in *self-defence*, to relax from this system; and every one now sees that the same motive prescribes that the commerce of the West Indies be wholly, and without restriction, thrown open to the people of the neighbouring continent, from which it has hitherto been shut out only by means of unnatural prohibitions.

We have said that the New World is the arbiter of the commercial policy of the Old; and we will now see in what way this is the fact in the case of our East Indian trade. Hitherto it has been the custom to impose discriminating duties in favour of the products of these colonies; and this, and this only, has given us the right to compel these dependencies, in return, to restrict themselves to the purchase of our manufactures. We have seen that this restrictive policy must be abandoned in the case of the West Indies and Canada, and still less shall we find it practicable to uphold it in the East. Our leading imports from this quarter must be cotton-wool, silk, indigo, and sugar. The last of these articles, as we have already shown in speaking of the West Indies, the Brazils have, by its successful culture, forced us to remove from the list of protected commodities; whilst the three first, being raw products, in the supply and manufacture of which we are so closely checkmated by the competition of the United States or of

---

* [These monopolies have, of course, long since been abolished.]

European countries, it would be madness to think of subjecting the fabrication of them to restrictive duties, however trifling.

We shall then be under the necessity of levying the same duties on the cotton, sugar, &c., imported from the East Indies, as on similar products coming from North or South America; and it will follow, of course, that, as we offer no privileges in our markets to the planters of Hindostan, we can claim none for our manufacturers in theirs. In other words, they must be left at liberty to buy wherever they can purchase cheapest, and to sell where they can do so at the dearest rate; they will, in all respects, be, commercially and fiscally speaking, the same to us as though they did not form a part of his Majesty's dominions. Where then will be the plea for subjecting ourselves to the heavy taxation required to maintain armies and navies for the defence of these colonies?

Provided our manufactures be cheaper than those of our rivals, we shall command the custom of these colonies by the same motives of self-interest which bring the Peruvians, the Brazilians, or the natives of North America, to clothe themselves with the products of our industry; and, on the other hand, they will gladly sell to us their commodities through the same all-powerful impulse, provided we offer for them a more tempting price than they will command in other markets.

We have thus hastily and incidentally glanced at a subject which we predict will speedily force itself upon the attention of our politicians; and we know of nothing that would be so likely to conduce to a diminution of our burdens, by reducing the charges of the army, navy, and ordnance (amounting to fourteen millions annually), as a proper understanding of our relative position with respect to our colonial possessions.* We are aware that no power was ever yet known, voluntarily, to give up the dominion over a part of its territory. But if it could be made manifest to the trading and industrious portions

* [The charges for army, navy, and ordnance, for the year 1865, amounted to £25,280,925.]

of this nation, who have no honours or interested ambition of any kind at stake in the matter, that whilst our dependencies are supported at an expense to them, in direct taxation, of more than five millions annually, they serve but as gorgeous and ponderous appendages to swell our ostensible grandeur, but in reality to complicate and magnify our government expenditure, without improving our balance of trade—surely under such circumstances, it would become at least a question for anxious inquiry with a people so overwhelmed with debt, whether those colonies should not be suffered to support and defend themselves as separate and independent existences.

Adam Smith, more than sixty years ago, promulgated his doubts of the wisdom and profitableness of our colonial policy —at a time, be it remembered, when we were excluded, by the mother countries, from the South American markets, and when our West Indian possessions appeared to superficial minds an indispensable source of vast wealth to the British empire. Had he lived to our day, to behold the United States of America, after freeing themselves from the dominion of the mother country, become our largest and most friendly commercial connection—had he lived also to behold the free states of South America only prevented from outstripping in magnitude all our other customers by the fetters which an absurd law of exclusive dealing with those very West Indian Colonies has imposed on our commerce—how fully must his opinions have coincided with all that we have urged on this subject !

Here, let us observe, that it is worthy of surprise how little progress has been made in the study of that science of which Adam Smith was, more than half a century ago, the great luminary. We regret that no society has been formed for the purpose of disseminating a knowledge of the just principles of trade. Whilst agriculture can boast almost as many associations as there are British counties; whilst every city in the kingdom contains its botanical, phrenological, or mechanical institutions, and these again possess their periodical journals (and not merely these, for even *war* sends forth its *United Service Magazine*), we possess no association of traders, united together for the common object of enlightening the world upon a question so little understood, and so loaded with obloquy, as free trade.

We have our Banksian, our Linnæan, our Hunterian Societies; and why should not at least our greatest commercial and manufacturing towns possess their Smithian Societies, devoted to the purpose of promulgating the beneficent truths of the " Wealth of Nations?" Such institutions, by promoting a correspondence with similar societies that would probably be organised abroad (for it is our example, in questions affecting commerce, that strangers follow), might contribute to the spread of liberal and just views of political science, and thus tend to ameliorate the restrictive policy of foreign governments, through the legitimate influence of the opinions of their people.

Nor would such societies be fruitless at home. Prizes might be offered for the best essays on the corn question; or lecturers might be sent to enlighten the agriculturists, and to invite discussion upon a subject so difficult and of such paramount interest to all.

The question of the policy or justice of prohibiting the export of machinery might be brought to the test of public discussion; these, and a thousand other questions might, with usefulness, engage the attention of such associations.

But to return to the consideration of the subject more immediately before us.

It will be seen from the arguments and facts we have urged, and are about to lay before our readers, that we entertain no fears that our interests would be likely to suffer from the aggrandisement of a Christian power at the expense of Turkey, even should that power be Russia. On the contrary, we have no hesitation in avowing it as our deliberate conviction, that not merely great Britain, but the entire civilised world, will have reason to congratulate itself, the moment when that territory again falls beneath the sceptre of any other European power whatever. Ages must elapse before its favoured region will become, as it is by nature destined to become, the seat and centre of commerce, civilisation and true religion ; but the first step towards this consummation must be to convert Constantinople again into that which every lover of humanity and peace longs to behold it—the capital of a Christian people. Nor let it be objected by more enlightened believers, that the Russians would plant that corrupted branch of our religion, the Greek Church, on the spot where the first Christian monarch erected a temple to the true faith of the Apostles. We are no advocates of that Church, with its idolatrous worship and pantomimic ceremonials, fit only to delude the most degraded and ignorant minds ; but we answer—put into a people's hands the Bible in lieu of the Koran—let the religion of Mahomet give place to that of Jesus Christ ; and human reason, aided by the printing press and the commerce of the world, will not fail to erase the errors which time, barbarism, or the cunning of its priesthood, may have engrafted upon it.

But to descend from these higher motives to the question of our own interests, to which, probably, as politicians, we ought to confine our consideration.

Nothing, we confess, appears so opposed to the facts of experience, as the belief which has been so industriously propagated in this country, that Russia, if she held the keys of the Dardanelles, would exclude all trade from the Black Sea and the Sea of Marmora. The writer so often quoted, says— " On the occupation of the Dardanelles disappears the importance of our possessions in the Levant. They were only valuable because the Turks held these Straits. When Russia is there, they are valueless, and will soon be untenable." It might be a sufficient reply to these assertions, unsupported by facts or reasoning, to demand of what use will these maritime possessions be to Russia, or any other power, unless for the purposes of trade ? Why did the government of St. Petersburg, for nearly a century, bend a steady and longing eye on the ports of the Euxine, but for the facilities which the possession of one of them would give to the traffic between the interior provinces of Russia and the Mediterranean?

We write, however, with no motive but to disabuse the public mind on an important question ; and as we prefer in all cases to appeal to facts, we shall here give a few particulars of the rise and progress of the only commercial port of conse-quence as yet established in the Black Sea.

The first stone of the town of Odessa was laid, by order of Catherine, in 1792.

Previously to this, the Euxine was so little visited by our mariners, that every kind of absurd story was advanced and credited respecting the danger of its navigation : the very name was held to be only synonymous with the black and dismal character of its storms, or the perilous mists that it was imagined constantly shrouded its surface. The Danube was, in a like spirit of credulity, suspected to pour from its channel so vast a deposit of mud as to fill the Black Sea with shoals, that threatened, in the course of a few ages, to convert its waters into dry land ; whilst this river, the noblest in Europe, sealed by Turkish jealousy, thus blotting out, as it were, from commercial existence, that vast pastoral district through which it flowed— this stream, whose course lay almost in the centre of Christendom, was as little known as the great yellow river of China.

Odessa has fully equalled the rapid commercial rise of St. Petersburg, to which only in importance it is now the second in the Russian empire. These two ports, which we are taught to believe belong to the most anti-commercial people, present, singularly enough, the two most astonishing instances in Europe of quick advances in wealth, trade, and population.

This town has latterly been declared a free port, with exemption from taxes ; and, therefore, we cannot but anticipate for it a much more rapid career in the time to come.

The population of Odessa is estimated at 40,000 souls. The

exportation of tallow has increased in two years twenty-fold, thus civilising and enriching extensive districts which must have remained in comparative barbarism, had not this outlet been found for their produce. During the same time the breed of sheep has been much improved in these vast southern regions of the Russian territory by the introduction of the merinoes, and the consequent increase of the export of wool has been very considerable.

The amount of imports is stated at 30,000,000 roubles.

We subjoin a statement of the movement of Russian and British shipping at this port, to show that here, as at St. Petersburg and elsewhere, the commerce of England finds a proportionate extension with the trade of other countries.

SHIPPING AT ODESSA.*

Vessels.	1826.		1827.		1828.		1829.		1830.		1831.	
	Arrived.	Sailed.	Arrived.	Sailed.	Arrived.	Sailed.	Arrived.	Sailed.	Arrived.	Sailed.	Arrived.	Sailed.
Russian.	164	111	167	122	50	38	24	38	172	194	155	136
British...	104	105	155	143	4	8	65	43	147	169	81	83

Already have its merchants appeared as our customers on the Exchange of Manchester; and it only requires that we remove our suicidal restrictions on the import of corn, to

* M'Culloch's Dictionary, p. 858; a work of unrivalled labour and usefulness, which ought to have a place in the library of every merchant or reader who feels interested in the commerce and statistics of the world. We will quote from another part of this valuable work, the opinion of the author upon the influences of Russian sway in this quarter :—" On the whole, however, a gradual improvement is taking place ; and whatever objections may, on other grounds, be made to the encroachments of Russia in this quarter, there can be no doubt that, by introducing comparative security and good order into the countries under her authority, she has materially improved their condition, and accelerated their progress to a more advanced state."—P. 1108.

render Odessa ultimately one of the chief contributors to the trade of Liverpool.

The influence of Russia, since she has gained a settlement on the shores of the Euxine, has been successfully exercised in throwing open the navigation of its waters, with those of the Danube, to the world ; and this noble river has at length been subjected to the dominion of steam, which will, beyond all other agents, tend most rapidly to bring the population of its banks within the pale of civilisation. A Danube Steam Navigation Joint Stock Company has been projected, and will, in all probability, be in operation next summer ; and, as this will give the route from the west of Europe to Turkey, by the way of Vienna, the preference, there is no reason to doubt that eventually this river will enjoy a considerable traffic both of passengers and merchandise.

We have probably said sufficient to prove, from facts, that Russia is not an anti-commercial nation.

We have endeavoured likewise to show that alarms for the safety of our eastern possessions ought not to induce us to go to war to check a movement three thousand miles removed from their capital ; and to those who are inspired with fear for our European commerce, from the aggrandisement of Russia, we have answered by showing that Napoleon, when he had all Europe at his feet, could not diminish our trade eight per cent.

What then remains to be urged in favour of the policy of this Government putting its over-taxed people to the cost of making warlike demonstrations in favour of Turkey ? At the moment when we write a British fleet is wintering in the Gulf of Vourla, the cost of which, at a low estimate, probably exceeds two millions, to say nothing of living *materiel;* and this is put in requisition in behalf of a country with which we carry on a commerce less in annual amount than is turned over by either of two trading concerns that we could name in the city of London !

But we are to await a regeneration of this Mahometan empire. Our arms, we are told, are not only to defend its territory, but to reorganise or reconstruct the whole Turkish government, and to bestow upon its subjects improved political institutions. Let us note what the pamphlet before us says upon this subject, and let it be borne in mind that the writer's sentiments have been applauded by some of our influential journals—" It is the policy of England which alone can save her : it is therefore no trivial or idle investigation which we have undertaken, since it is her political elements that we have to embody into a new political instrument."—P. 54. Again—" In the capital, in the meanest villages, in the centre of communications, on the furthest frontiers, a feeling of vague but intense expectation is spread, which will not be satisfied with less *at our hands* than internal reorganisation and external independence."—P. 62. Again—" Unless anticipated by visible intervention on the part of England, which will relieve them from the permanent menace of the occupation of the capital, and which *will impose on the Government* (*!*) the necessity of a change of measures, a catastrophe is inevitable."—P. 63. And again—"An empire which in extent, in resources, in population, in position, and in individual qualities and courage—in all, in fact, save instruction—is one of the greatest on the face of the earth, is brought to look with ardent expectation for the arrival of a foreign squadron, and a body of auxiliaries in its capital, and to expect from their presence *the reformation of internal abuses* (*!*) and the restoration of its political independence."—P. 73.

To protect Turkey against her neighbour, Russia—to defend the Turks against their own government — to force on the latter a constitution, we suppose—to redress all internal grievances in a state where there is no law but despotism ! Here, then, in a word, is the *"trifling succour"* (p. 2) which we are called on to render our ancient ally; and if the people of Great Britain desired to add another couple of hundreds of millions to their debt, we think a scheme is discovered by which they may be gratified, without seeking for quarrels in any other quarter.

If such propositions as these are, however, to be received gravely, it might be suggested to inquire, would Russia, would Austria, remain passive, whilst another power sent her squadrons and her armies from ports a thousand miles distant to take possession of the capital and supersede the government of their adjoining neighbour ?   Would there be no such thing as Russian or Austrian jealousy of British aggrandisement, and might not our Quixotic labours in behalf of Mahometan re-generation be possibly perplexed by the co-operation of those Powers?   These questions present to us the full extent of the dilemma in which we must be placed, if we ever attempt an internal interference with the Ottoman territory.   *Without* the consent and assistance of Russia and Austria, we should not be allowed to land an army in that country.   We might, it is true, blockade the Dardanelles, and thus at any time annihilate the trade of Constantinople and the Black Sea.   But our interests would suffer by such a step ; and the object of inter-meddling at all is, of course, to benefit, and not destroy our trade.   We must, then, if we would remodel Turkey, act in conjunction with Russia, Austria, and France.   Would the two former of these powers be likely to lend a very sincere and disinterested co-operation, or must we prepare for a game of intrigues and protocols ? *

* We here give an extract from the correspondence of a London morning paper, upon the affairs of Greece, that is illustrative of the case in hand :—

"*Nauplia, Nov.* 28, 1834.—If we (the English people) had not been paying for fleets, destroyers of fleets, protocols, loans, extraordinary ambassadors, presidents, couriers, subsidies, &c., in the Levant, we might not have been surprised at the present state of things.   But taking into account the talents of Palmerston and S. Canning, and the straightforward, open, John Bull policy of their agent here, really it is wonderful how they can have allowed the other powers to have made such a mess of the business.   But the worst part of the affair is, that things are quite as complicated now as they were a week after the breaking out of the Revolution.   Here we have a fleet reaching from Gibraltar

These are the probable consequences of our interposing in the case of Turkey ; and, from the danger of which, the only alternative lies in a strict neutrality. We are aware that it would be a novel case for England to remain passive, whilst a struggle was going on between two European powers ; and we know, also, that there is a predilection for continental politics amongst the majority of our countrymen, that would render it extremely difficult for any administration to preserve peace under such circumstances. Public opinion must undergo a change ; our ministers must no longer be held responsible for the every-day political quarrels all over Europe ; nor, when an opposition member of Parliament, or an opposition journalist,* wishes to assail a foreign secretary, must he be suffered to taunt him with neglect of the honour of Great Britain, if he should prudently abstain from involving her in the dissensions that afflict distant communities.

to the Dardanelles—here we have the Russians as busy as ever—and here we have *not* the proceeds of the loan which our (the British) Government has guaranteed, nor have we a revenue that will pay the interest of it." Amusingly enough, we find, in another column of the very same copy of the same journal, a letter from its correspondent, dated at Constantinople, Nov. 25, from which the following is extracted :—" Now is the time to step forward ; a cracking south-wester and a bold front are all that would be wanted ; and our ships once at anchor in the Bosphorus, adieu to the ambitious views of Russia ! They would burst like a child's bubble. Adieu to the stupid notions about the inevitable dissolution of Turkey. Adieu to the accursed treaty which binds lovely Turkey to a remorseless ravager ! * * * One of her vain finesses is now visible in Austria, where a hired press would make the world believe that Austria is seriously opposed to Russian schemes. It does not require a very long or sharp look-out to see that the two absolute governments are acting in collusion. * * * It is a pretty manœuvre to lead us from the real point of attack — a mere feint ; we must pay no attention to it, but direct all our strength and energy to the true point, Constantinople; that Constantinople which, once in Russia's hands, becomes the mistress of Europe."

* Extract from a London paper, *October* 22, 1834 :— " As at home, so abroad ; the Whigs have failed in all their negotiations, and not one question have they settled, except the passing of a Reform Bill and a Poor Law Bill. The Dutch question is undecided ; the French are still at Ancona ; Don Carlos is fighting in Spain ; Don Miguel and his adherents are preparing for a new conflict in Portugal ; Turkey and Egypt are at daggers drawn ; Switzerland is

There is no remedy for this but in the wholesome exercise of the people's opinion in behalf of their own interests. The middle and industrious classes of England can have no interest apart from the preservation of peace. The honours, the fame, the emoluments of war belong not to them ; the battle-plain is the harvest-field of the aristocracy, watered with the blood of the people.

We know of no means by which a body of members in the reformed House of Commons could so fairly achieve for itself the patriotic title of a national party, as by associating for the common object of deprecating all intervention on our part in continental politics. Such a party might well comprise every representative of our manufacturing and commercial districts, and would, we doubt not, very soon embrace the majority of a powerful House of Commons. At some future election, we may probably see the test of "*no foreign politics*" applied to those who offer to become the representatives of free con-stituencies. Happy would it have been for us, and well for our posterity, had such a feeling predominated in this country fifty years ago ! But although, since the peace, we have profited so little by the bitter experience of the revolutionary wars as to seek a participation in all the subsequent continental squabbles, and though we are bound by treaties, or involved in guarantees, with almost every state of Europe; still the coming moment is only the more proper for adopting the true path of national policy, which always lies open to us.

We say the coming moment is only the more fit for with-drawing ourselves from foreign politics ; and surely there are

---

quarrelling with her neighbouring states about Italian refugees; Frankfort is occupied by Prussian troops, in violation of the treaty of Vienna ; Algiers is being made a large French colony, in violation of the promises made to the contrary by France in 1829 and 1830 ; ten thousand Polish nobles are still pro-scribed and wandering in Europe; French gaols are full of political offenders, who, when liberated or acquitted, will begin again to conspire. In one word, nothing is terminated." It is plain that, if this writer had his will, the Whigs would leave nothing in the world for Providence to attend to.

signs in Europe that fully justify the sentiment. With France, still in the throes of her last revolution, containing a generation of young and ardent spirits, without the resources of commerce, and therefore burning for the excitement and employment of war; with Germany, Prussia, Hungary, Austria,* and Italy, all dependent for tranquillity upon the fragile bond of attachment of their subjects to a couple of aged paternal monarchs; with Holland and Belgium, each sword in hand; and with Turkey, not so much yielding to the pressure of Russia, as sinking beneath an inevitable religious and political destiny—surely, with such elements of discord as these fermenting all over Europe, it becomes more than ever our duty to take natural shelter from a storm, from entering into which we could hope for no benefits, but might justly dread renewed sacrifices.

Nor do we think it would tend less to promote the ulterior benefit of our continental neighbours than our own, were Great Britain to refrain from participating in the conflicts that may arise around her. An onward movement of constitutional liberty must continue to be made by the less advanced nations of Europe, so long as one of its greatest families holds out the example of liberal and enlightened freedom. England, by calmly directing her undivided energies to the purifying of her own internal institutions, to the emancipation of her commerce —above all, to the unfettering of her press from its excise bonds—would, by thus serving as it were for the beacon of other nations, aid more effectually the cause of political progression all over the continent than she could possibly do by plunging herself into the strife of European wars.

For, let it never be forgotten, that it is not by means of war that states are rendered fit for the enjoyment of constitutional freedom; on the contrary, whilst terror and bloodshed reign in the land, involving men's minds in the extremities of hopes and fears, there can be no process of thought, no education going on, by which alone can a people be prepared for

* Since writing this, the death of the Emperor of Austria is announced.

the enjoyment of rational liberty. Hence, after a struggle of twenty years, *begun in behalf of freedom*, no sooner had the wars of the French revolution terminated, than all the nations of the continent fell back again into their previous state of political servitude, and from which they have, ever since the peace, been *qualifying* to rescue themselves, by the gradual process of intellectual advancement. Those who, from an eager desire to aid civilisation, wish that Great Britain should interpose in the dissensions of neighbouring states, would do wisely to study, in the history of their own country, how well a people can, by the force and virtue of native elements, and without external assistance of any kind, work out their own political regeneration : they might learn too, by their own annals, that it is only when at peace with other states that a nation finds the leisure for looking within itself, and discovering the means to accomplish great domestic ameliorations.

To those generous spirits we would urge, that, in the present day, commerce is the grand panacea, which, like a beneficent medical discovery, will serve to inoculate with the healthy and saving taste for civilisation all the nations of the world. Not a bale of merchandise leaves our shores, but it bears the seeds of intelligence and fruitful thought to the members of some less enlightened community; not a merchant visits our seats of manufacturing industry, but he returns to his own country the missionary of freedom, peace, and good government—whilst our steamboats, that now visit every port of Europe, and our miraculous railroads, that are the talk of all nations, are the advertisements and vouchers for the value of our enlightened institutions.

In closing this part of our task, we shall only add, that, whatever other plea may in future be allowed to induce us to embark in a continental conflict, we trust we have proved, that so far as our commerce is concerned, it can neither be sustained nor greatly injured abroad by force or violence. The foreign customers who visit our markets are not brought hither through fear of the power or the influence of British diplomatists : they are not captured by our fleets and armies : and as little are they attracted by feelings of love for us ; for that "there is no friendship in trade" is a maxim equally applicable to nations and to individuals. It is solely from the promptings of self-interest that the merchants of Europe, as of the rest of the world, send their ships to our ports to be freighted with the products of our labour. The self-same impulse drew all nations, at different periods of history, to Tyre, to Venice, and to Amsterdam ; and if, in the revolution of time and events, a country should be found (which is probable) whose cottons and woollens shall be cheaper than those of England and the rest of the world, then to that spot—even should it, by supposition, be buried in the remotest nook of the globe—will all the traders of the earth flock ; and no human power, no fleets or armies, will prevent Manchester, Liverpool, and Leeds, from sharing the fate of their once proud predecessors in Holland, Italy, and Phœnicia.*

* Lest it might be said that we are advocating Russian objects of ambition, we think it necessary to observe, that we trust the entire spirit of this pamphlet will show that we are not of *Russian politics.* Our sole aim is the *just interests* of England, regardless of the objects of other nations.

IRELAND.

WHILST within the last twenty years our sympathies have gone forth over the whole of Europe in quest of nations suffering from, or rising up against the injustice of their rulers; whilst Italy, Greece, Spain, France, Portugal, Turkey, Belgium, and Poland, have successively filled the newspapers with tales of their domestic wrongs; and whilst our diplomatists, fleets, and armies have been put in motion at enormous cost, to carry our counsel, or, if needful, our arms, to the assistance of the people of these remote regions; it is an unquestionable fact, that the population of a great portion of our own empire has, at the same time, presented a grosser spectacle of moral and physical debasement than is to be met with in the whole civilised world.

If an intelligent foreigner, after having travelled through England, Scotland, and Wales, and enjoyed the exhibition of wealth, industry, and happiness, afforded everywhere by the population of these realms, were, when upon the eve of departing for the shores of Ireland, to be warned of the scenes of wretchedness and want that awaited him in that country, he would naturally assume the cause in some such question as this :—" The people are no doubt indolent, and destitute of the energy that belongs to the English character ? " If it were answered, that, so far from such being the case, the Irish are the hardiest labourers on earth; that the docks and canals of England, and the railroads of America are the produce of their toil; in short, that they are the hewers of wood and the drawers of water for other nations—then the next inquiry from this stranger would probably be in some such form as this :—" But their soil no doubt is barren, and their climate inhospitable : nature has besides, probably, denied to them the rivers and harbours which are essential to commerce ? " What would be his surprise to be answered, that, in natural fertility, and in the advantages of navigable streams, lakes, and harbours, Ireland is more favoured than England, Scotland, or Wales.*

Where, then, shall we seek for the causes of the poverty and barbarism that afflict this land ? How shall we be able to account for the fact, that commerce and civilisation, which have from the earliest ages journeyed westward, and in their course have even stayed to enrich the marshes of the Adriatic and the fens of Holland, should have passed over in their flight to the New World a spot more calculated by nature than almost any other besides, to be the seat of a great internal and external trade ?

We do not profess to be able to disclose all the precise causes of the depressed fate of Ireland ; still less do we pretend to offer a panacea for all the ills that afflict her. Our object in introducing the subject here is, to show the absurdity and injustice of that policy which leads us to seek amongst other nations for objects of compassion and care, and to neglect the urgent demands that are made upon us at our very door.

The strongest ground of grievance that we have ever heard alleged against us by intelligent Irishmen, unimbued with party feelings, is the total neglect and ignorance of their country that

* " And sure it is yet a most beautiful and sweet country as any is under heaven, being stored throughout with many goodly rivers, replenished with all sorts of fish most abundantly, sprinkled with many very sweet islands and goodly lakes, like inland seas that will carry even shippes upon their waters ; adorned with goodly woods, even fit for building of houses and shippes so commodiously, as that, if some princes in the world had them, they would soon hope to be lords of all the seas, of all the world ; also full of very good ports and havens opening upon England, as inviting us to come into them, to see what excellent commodities that country can afford ; besides, the soyle itselfe fit to yeeld all kinde of fruit that shall be committed thereunto. And lastly, the heavens most mild and temperate, though somewhat more moist than the parts towards the east."—*Spenser.*

prevail amongst the people of England. To the middle classes of this country, as to an impartial tribunal, untainted by the venom of their political and religious factions, a large portion of the Irish people look for the probable regeneration of their unhappy country. Without this tardy effort of justice at our hands, they will never be able to escape from the vortex of their social distractions. This patriotic party, including so much of the intelligence and industry of Ireland, claim from their fellow-subjects on this side of the Channel (and they have a right to claim it), such a consideration of their country, its population and resources, its history, institutions, and geography—in fact, just such a study of Ireland as shall give them a knowledge of its anomalous physical and moral state.

It is almost incredible how little is known of this, one of the largest both in area and population, of the four divisions of the kingdom. Let any one of our readers take a person of average intelligence, and ask him which is the finest river of the United Kingdom; he will answer, probably, the Thames, the Humber, or the Severn; it is ten to one against his naming the Shannon.

We will venture to say that there are as many individuals in England conversant with the city of New York and the course of the Hudson, as there are who are acquainted with the topography of Limerick, and the banks of the largest river in the British Empire.

The past fate of Ireland, like the present condition of its people—presents to our view an anomaly that has no parallel in the history of nations. During all that period of time which has sufficed to bring the other states in Europe to emerge from barbarism—some to attain their zenith of glory, and again decay, others to continue at the summit of prosperity—Ireland has never enjoyed one age of perfect security or peace. She has, consequently, unlike every other nation, no era of literature, commerce, or the arts to boast of; nay, she does not exhibit, in her annals, an instance in which she has put forth in war a combined force to merit even the savage honours of military or naval fame.

Poets have feigned a golden age for this, as for every other country; but it never existed except in the pages of romance. Ireland never was, at any known period of her history, more tranquil or happy than at this day. She has from the first been the incessant prey of discord, bloodshed, and famine.

We, who are fond of digging deep into the foundations of causes, incline to assign as one reason of the adverse condition of this island, the circumstance of the Romans never having colonised it. That people, by deposing the petty chiefs, and gathering and compressing their septs into one communion— by inoculating the natives with a love of discipline—by depositing amongst them the seeds of the arts, and imparting a taste for civilisation—would probably have given to them that unity and consistency, as one people, the want of which has been the principal source of all their weakness and misfortune. Had the Romans occupied for three centuries such a country as this, they would perhaps have left it, on their departure from Britain, more advanced in all respects than it proved to be in the sixteenth century.

But whatever were the causes of the early degradation of this country, there can be no doubt that England has, during the last two centuries, by discouraging the commerce of Ireland —thus striking at the very root of civilisation—rendered herself responsible for much of the barbarism that at the present day afflicts it.

However much the conduct of England towards the sister island, in this particular, may have been dwelt upon for party purposes, it is so bad as scarcely to admit of exaggeration.

The first restrictions put upon the Irish trade were in the reign of Charles II.; and from that time down to the era when the United Volunteers of Ireland stepped forward to rescue their country from its oppressors (the only incident, by the way, in the chronicles of Ireland, deserving the name of a really national effort), our policy was directed incessantly to the destruction of the foreign trade of that country. Every attempt at manufacturing industry, with one exception, was likewise mercilessly nipped in the bud. Her natural capabilities might, for example, have led the people to the making of glass ; it was enacted that no glass should be allowed to be exported from Ireland, and its importation, except from England, was also prohibited. Her soil calculated for the pasturing of sheep, would have yielded wool equal to the best English qualities ; an absolute prohibition was laid on its exportation, and King William, in addressing the British Parliament, declared that he would " do everything in his power to discourage the woollen manufacture of Ireland." Down to the year 1779, we find that the export of woollen goods from that island remained wholly interdicted.

Not only was her commerce with the different ports of Europe fettered by the imposition of restrictions upon every valuable product that could interfere with the prosperity of England ; not only was all trade with Asia and the east of Europe excluded by the charters which were granted to the companies of London ; but her ports were actually sealed against the trade of the American colonies. Although Ireland presented to the ships of North America the nearest and the noblest havens in Europe, and appeared to be the natural landing-place for the products of the New World, her people were deprived of all benefit—nay, they were actually made to suffer loss and inconvenience from their favoured position ; laws were passed, prohibiting the importation of American commodities into Ireland, without first landing them in some port of England or Wales, whilst the export of Irish products to the colonies, excepting through some British port, was also interdicted.

If we add to this, that a law was enacted, preventing beef or live cattle from being exported to England, some idea may be formed of the commercial policy of this country towards

Ireland—a policy savouring more of the mean and sordid tyranny of the individual huckster over his poorer rival, than of any nobler oppression that is wont to characterise the acts of victorious nations.

Need we wonder that at this moment the entire foreign commerce of Ireland does not much exceed the trade of one second-rate port of Scotland ?*

There are those who think the Irish genius is unsuited to that eager and persevering pursuit of business which distinguishes the English people ; and they argue that, but for this, the natives of a region in all respects so favourable to commerce must have triumphed over the obstacles that clogged their industry.

There is, we believe, one cause existing, less connected with the injustice of England, and to which we are about to allude, why Ireland is below us, and other Protestant nations, in the scale of civilisation ; yet, if we look to the prosperity of her staple manufacture—the only industry that was tolerated by the Government of this country—it warrants the presumption that, under similar favouring circumstances, her woollens, or, indeed, her cottons, might, equally with her linens, have survived a competition with the fabrics of Great Britain.

But there exists, apart from all intolerant or party feelings on the question, a cause, and we believe a primary one, of the retrograde position, as compared with England and Scotland, in which we find Ireland at the present day, in the circumstance of the Roman Catholic religion being the faith of its people. Let us not be misunderstood—our business does not lie in polemics, and far be it from us to presume to decide which mode of worship may be most acceptable to the great Author of our being. We wish to speak only of the tendency, which, judging from facts that are before us, this Church has to retard the *secular* prosperity of nations.

Probably there is no country in which the effects of the

* Dundee.

Catholic and Reformed religions upon the temporal career of communities may be more fairly tested than in Switzerland. Of twenty-two cantons, ten are, in the majority of the population, Catholic ; eight Protestant ; and the remaining four are mixed, in. nearly equal proportions, of Protestants and Catholics. Those cantons in which the Catholic faith prevails are wholly pastoral in their pursuits, possessing no commerce or manufacturing industry beyond the rude products of domestic labour. Of the mixed cantons, three* are engaged in the manufacture of cotton ; and it is a remarkable feature in the industry of these, that the Catholic portion of their population is wholly addicted to agricultural, and the Protestant section to commercial pursuits. All the eight Protestant cantons are, more or less, engaged in manufactures.

Nor must we omit to add, which every traveller in Switzerland will have seen, that, in the education of the people, the cleanliness of the towns, the commodiousness of the inns, and the quality of the roads, the Protestant cantons possess a great superiority over their Catholic neighbours ; whilst such is the difference in the value of land, that an estate in Friburg, a Catholic canton, possessing a richer soil than that of Berne, from which it is divided only by a rivulet, is worth one-third less than the same extent of property in the latter Protestant district.

Such are the circumstances, as we find them in comparing one portion of the Swiss territory with another. The facts are still more striking if we view them in relation to the States immediately around them.

Switzerland, being an inland district far removed from the sea, is compelled to resort to Havre, Genoa, or Frankfort for the supply of the raw materials of her industry, which are transported by land three, four, or five hundred miles, *through Catholic States,* for the purpose of fabrication ; and the goods are afterwards reconveyed to the same ports for exportation

* Appenzell, St. Gall, and Aargau.

to America or the Levant, where, notwithstanding this heavy expense of transit, and although Switzerland possesses no mineral advantages, they sustain a prosperous competition with their more favoured, but less industrious, neighbours and rivals.

If we refer to France, we shall find that a large depôt of manufacturing industry has been formed upon the extreme inland frontier of her territory on the Rhine, where her best cottons are fabricated and printed, and conveyed to the metropolis, about three hundred miles off, for sale. Alsace, the Protestant district we allude to, contains no local advantages, no iron or coals ; it is upwards of four hundred miles distant from the port through which the raw materials of its manufactures are obtained, and whence they are conveyed, entirely by land, passing through Paris, to which city the goods are destined to be again returned. Thus are these commodities transported, overland, more than seven hundred miles, for no other assignable reason, except that they may be subjected to the labour of Protestant hands.

Germany gives us additional facts to the same purport. It we divide this empire into north and south, we shall find the former, containing Prussia, Saxony, &c., to be chiefly Protestant, and to comprise nearly all the manufacturing and commercial interests of the country ; whilst the latter are principally Catholic, and almost wholly addicted to agriculture. Education, likewise, follows the same law here as in Switzerland ; for, whilst the Catholics amount to about twenty millions, and possess but five universities, the Protestants support thirteen, with only a population of fourteen millions.

If we turn to Catholic Italy, where there is very little manufacturing of any kind, we yet find that the commerce of the country is principally in the hands of foreigners. The merchants of Genoa, Naples, Trieste, &c., are chiefly British, Swiss, or Germans, whose houses, again, have their own agents in the principal interior cities ; so that the trade of the Italian States is in great part transacted by Protestants. We need scarcely add to these statements the fact, which all are acquainted with, that, in Ireland, the staple manufacture is almost wholly confined to the Protestant province.

We shall probably be reminded of the former commercial grandeur of Spain and the Italian republics. This was, however, to a great extent, the effect of monopolies, which must, from their nature, be of transient benefit to nations, and, moreover, they flourished prior to the complete triumph of the Reformation ; and our object is merely to exhibit a comparison between Protestant and Catholic communities of the same period. Besides, Spain and Italy have left no evidences of the enlightened industry of their people—such as are to be seen, for example, to attest the energy of the Dutch, in the canals and dykes of Holland.

We have thus briefly glanced at the comparative conditions of the Catholic and Protestant interests in Europe ; and, disclaiming, as we do, any theological purpose, we trust we may demand for our argument, what is not often accorded to this invidious topic, the candid attention of our readers. The above facts, then, go far to prove that, in human affairs at least, the Reformed faith conduces more than Catholicism to the prosperity of nations.

We shall not argue that the welfare of States, any more than of individuals, affords proofs of spiritual superiority ; we will admit that it does not ; but, if it can be proved from facts (as we think even our intelligent and ingenuous Roman Catholic readers will agree we have done) that the Protestant is, more than the Catholic faith, conducive to the growth of national riches and intelligence, then there must be acknowledged to exist a cause, independent of misgovernment, for the present state of Ireland, as compared with that of Great Britain, for which England cannot be held altogether responsible.

The deficient education of a people is, no doubt, a circumstance that must tend, in these days, when the physical sciences and the arts are so intimately blended with manufacturing industry, and when commerce itself has become a branch of philosophy, to keep them in the rear rank of civilised nations ; but we think the abhorrence of change that characterises Catholic states, and which we shall find not merely to affect religious observances, but to pervade all the habits of social life, has even a more powerful influence over their destinies.

In proof of this, if we take the pages of Cervantes and Le Sage, and compare the portraits and scenes they have depicted, with the characters, costumes, and customs of the present day, we shall find that the Spanish people are, after the lapse of so many ages, in even the minutest observances, wholly un-changed. On the other hand, if we look into Shakespeare, or examine the canvas of Teniers, we shall find that, during the same interval of time, the populations of Holland and England have been revolutionised in all the modes of life, so as scarcely to leave one national feature of those ages for recognition in our day.

Ireland has clung tenaciously to her characteristics of ancient days.

"There is a great use among the Irish," says Spenser, writing more than two hundred years ago, " to make great assemblies together upon a rath or hill, there to parley, as they say, about matters and wrongs between township and town-ship, or one private person and another."—Vol. viii. p. 399. Now, no person could, by possibility, pass six months in the south of Ireland, during the present year, but he would be certain to witness some gatherings of this nature. But who, that has travelled in that island, can have failed to be struck with that universal feature in the dress of the people—the great-coat ? " He maketh his mantle," says Spenser, speaking of the Irish peasant of his time, " his house; and under it covereth himself from the wrath of heaven, from the offence of the earth, and from the sight of men. When it raineth it is his pent-house ; when it bloweth, it is his tent; when it freezeth, it is his tabernacle. In summer, he can wear it loose ; in winter, he can wrap it close ; at all times, he can use it ; never heavy, never cumbersome."—P. 367. We have ourselves seen the Irish of our own day, in the midst of winter, wrapping the mantle close, and we have seen them spreading it loosely in summer ; we have seen the peasant, whilst at plough, obliged to quit one of the stilts every minute for the purpose of adjusting the great-coat that was tucked clumsily round his loins ; and we have beheld the labourer at work, with his mantle thrown inconveniently over his arms and shoulders ; but we have never witnessed it thrown aside. In truth, it is still the mantle that " hides him from the sight of men; " for, like charity, it cloaks a multitude of defects in the garments beneath.

But it is not in mere externals that we shall find the character of Irish society unchanged. In the manifestations of the passions, in the vehement displays of natural feeling, there is, amidst the general amelioration of the surrounding world, alas ! no improvement here. To quote again from the pages of Spenser, an eye-witness :—" I saw an old woman, which was his foster-mother, take up his head, whilst he was quartered, and sucked up all the bloode that runne thereoute, saying, that the earthe was not worthy to drinke it ; and therewith, also steeped her face and breast, and tore her hair, crying out and shrieking most terribly."—*Ibid.* p. 381.

Let us compare the above scene, which was enacted at the execution of one of the turbulent natives of the sixteenth century, with the following incident that occurred at the late Rathcormac tithe tragedy :—

" I went up to inspect the haggart where the carnage occurred, and so awful a spectacle I never witnessed ; the straw, all saturated with human gore, so that blood oozed through on the pressure of the foot ; and, shocking to relate, the widow Collins was seen to kiss the blood of her sons, imprecating God's vengeance on the murderers of her children."—*Dub. Ev. Post, Dec.* 23, 1834.

Who would imagine that more than two centuries have elapsed between the dates when these parallel occurrences took place in one and the same country?

Viewing, as we confessedly do, the Roman Catholic religion to be a great operating cause against the amelioration of the state of Ireland, it becomes an interesting question, how it happens that we find its dogmas to be professed with so much zeal at the present day in that country. How does it arise, that whereas, during the last three centuries, history exhibits nation after nation yielding up its religion to those reforms which time had rendered necessary, until nearly the whole of northern and western Europe has become Protestant —Ireland, notwithstanding so much contiguous change, still clings, with greater devotion than ever, to the shattered tiara of Rome? That such is the case is proved by the evidence of a trustworthy author, whose recent travels in Ireland we shall have occasion to allude to.*

We fervently believe that persecution—perhaps honestly devised, but still persecution—has done for this Church what, under the circumstances, nothing besides could have achieved; it has enabled it to resist, not only unscathed, but actually with augmented power, the shocks of a free press, and the liberalising influence of the freest constitutional government in Europe.

We shall be told that the epithet persecution no longer applies, since all civil disabilities are removed from our Catholic fellow-subjects; but, we ask, does it not still apply as much in principle, though not in degree, to the present condition of the

* " In no country is there more bigotry and superstition among the lower orders, or more blind obedience to the priesthood ; in no country is there so much intolerance and zeal among the ministers of religion. I do believe, that at this moment Catholic Ireland is more rife for the re-establishment of the Inquisition than any other country in Europe."—*Inglis' Travels in Ireland.* See the same traveller's description of Patrick's Purgatory, Loch Dergh. It adds weight to the testimony of this writer upon such a subject, when it is recollected that he is the author of " Travels in Spain."

Irish Church—where six millions of Catholics are forced to see the whole tithe of their soil possessed by the clergy of one million of Protestants—as it did to the persecutions of the ancient martyrs, or to the auto-da-fés of modern Spain? Is not the spirit of persecution the same, but modified to meet the spirit of the age?

If we would bring this case home to our own feelings, let us suppose that the arms of the United States of America were to achieve the conquest of Great Britain; we will further suppose that that country possessed an established church differing in faith from our own—for instance, let it be imagined to be of the Unitarian creed. Now, then, we put it to the feelings of our countrymen, would they, or would they not, regard it as persecution, if they saw the whole of the tithes of England diverted from their present uses, to be applied to the support of a faith which they abhorred? Would it not be felt as persecution to be compelled, not only to behold their cathedrals and churches in the hands of the ministers of a (by them) detested creed, but the lands and revenues which appertained to them, wrested from their present purposes, by the force of a Government on the other side of the ocean? And, seeing these things, would it not be felt and suffered as persecution, if the people of England, still clinging to a man to their national Church, were impelled by conscience to erect other temples of worship, and out of their own pockets to maintain their ejected and despised ministers?

But to come to the still more important question, we appeal to the breasts of our readers, would they, under such circumstances, be likely to become converts to the religion of their spoilers and oppressors? or would they not more probably nourish such a spirit of resentment and indignation as would render impossible a calm or impartial examination of its dogmas? And would not their children and their children's children be taught to abhor, even before they could understand, the very name of Unitarianism? But, pursuing our hypothesis, supposing all this to occur in England, and that the nation were compelled, by the presence of a sufficient army, to submit—what would the probable effects of such a state of things be upon the peace and prosperity of the community ? However excellent might be the laws and institutions, however liberal and enlightened the policy, in other respects, of the government set over us by the Americans, whatever commercial advantages might be derived from a complete incorporation with the United States—would the people, the church-loving people of those realms, be found to be quietly and successfully pursuing their worldly callings, forgetting the grievances of their consciences? We hope not! For the honour of our countrymen we fervently believe that all worldly pursuits and interests would be, by them, and their sons, and their sons' sons, even down to the tenth generation, abandoned; that agitation would be rife in the land, and that every county in England would put forth its O'Connell, wielding the terrible energies of combined freemen, until the time that saw such monstrous tyranny abated !

Persecution may be, as it often has been, the buttress of error ; but all history proves that it can never aid the cause of truth.

What has preserved the Jews a distinct people, scattered as they have been amidst all the nations of the earth ? No miracle, certainly ; for they are now dissolving into the ranks of Christians before the sun of American toleration ; * and our country, but especially the spot where we write, gives us a similar beneficent example in comparison with other States. Nothing more than the universal and unintermitted series of oppressions that characterised the conduct of every Government towards that despised people, from the destruction of

* In the United States a Jew can hold all offices of State ; he may by law become the Chancellor of the Exchequer, Chief Justice, or even President. An American naval commander of the Hebrew faith was, upon one occasion, introduced to George IV.

Jerusalem down to the last century, can be necessary to account for the fact that the Hebrew people exceed, perhaps, at this moment, in numbers, the population of Judæa at the most flourishing period of its history.   Nor, if it were desired, during the eighteen centuries to come, to preserve the Jews a separate people, could the wit or the philosophy of man devise a scheme to prevent their amalgamating with the nations of the earth, other than by persevering in the same infallible course of persecution.

Let them search the annals of religious persecution (and it is the most humiliating chapter in the history of poor human nature), and we will challenge the advocates of coercive deal-ings in matters of conscience to produce an instance where violence, bribery, or secular power in any form, has ever aided the cause of true religion.   To the honour of the immaterial portion of our being, although the body may be made to yield to these influences, the soul, disdaining all mortal fetters, owes no allegiance but to itself and its Maker.

So long, then, as the Church of England possesses the whole of the religious revenue of Ireland, there cannot be— nay, judging of the case as our own, there ought not to be —peace or prosperity for its people ; and, what is of still more vital importance, there can be, judging by the same rule, no chance of the dissemination of religious truth in that country.

Let us not be met by those unthinking persons who view tithes as religion, with the cry about the destruction of the Protestant Church ; we are of that Church ; and we reckon it amongst the happiest circumstances of our destiny that Providence has placed us in a Protestant land.   In our opinion—and we have endeavoured to prove it from the homely, but incontrovertible arguments of facts—no greater temporal misfortune can attach to a people of the present age than to profess the Roman Catholic religion ; and it is in order to give the Irish an oppor-tunity of considering with that *indifferency* which we believe

with Locke is the indispensable prelude to the successful search
after truth, the doctrines of our reformed faith, that we would
do them the justice, in the first place, of putting them on a
perfectly equal footing, as respects matters of conscience, with
their Protestant fellow-subjects.

We are not visionary enough to shut our eyes to the vast
impediments in the way of such a consummation as we have
jumped to. These, however, do not in the least affect the
question as to its justice or expediency. The obstacles lie in
the House of Peers, and probably in the breast of the King.
If the conscience of the latter should be affected with scruples
as to the binding nature of the coronation oath, precautions
might be taken to prevent a similar future obstacle on the
demise of the crown. With respect to the House of Lords,
difficulties of a less august nature will have to be encountered ;
for why should the fact be concealed, that the Church question, in whichever way agitated, is one that concerns the
interests of the aristocracy ? Hence is the difficulty : that,
whereas, we sincerely believe, if a canvass were made from
house to house throughout Great Britain, four-fifths of the
middle classes of its people would be found at once not interested in the temporalities of the Irish Church, and willing
to grant to their Catholic fellow-subjects of Ireland a complete
equality of religious privileges ; on the contrary, if an appeal
were to be made to the votes of the House of Peers, four-fifths
of that assembly would very likely oppose such a measure of
justice and peace ; and probably that great majority of its members would be found to be, immediately or remotely, interested
in the revenues of that Church.

We would recommend the most ample concessions to be
made to countervail the obstacles of self-interest. There is no
present sacrifice of a pecuniary nature that will not be an ultimate gain to the middle and working classes of England, if it
only tend to pacify and regenerate Ireland.

Viewing the subject as a question of pounds, shillings, and

pence (and it partakes a great deal more of that character than folks are aware of), the people of England would be gainers by charging the whole amount of the Church revenue of Ireland to the Consolidated Fund, if by so doing they were only to escape the expense of supporting an enormous army * for the service of that country.

But we are, from another motive of self-interest, far more deeply concerned in the tranquillity and improvement of the sister kingdom : for it ought to be borne in view, and impressed upon the minds of the industrious classes of this country, that, unless we can succeed in laying the foundations of some plan for elevating the people of Ireland to an equality with us, they will inevitably depress us to a level with themselves. *There cannot permanently be, in a free community, two distinct castes or conditions of existence, such as are now to be found in this united empire.* Already is the process of assimilation going on ; and the town in which we write furnishes, amongst others, a striking example of the way in which the contagion of Irish habits is contaminating, whilst the competition of that people is depressing, the working classes of Britain.

Manchester is supposed to contain fifty thousand Irish, or

* Stations of the British Army in Ireland, on the 1st November, 1834. (*From the United Service Journal.*) Those marked thus * are depots of Regiments. 3rd Dragoon Guards, Dublin ; 4th Dragoon Guards, Cork ; 7th Dragoon Guards, Limerick ; 9th Lancers, Newbridge ; 10th Hussars, Dundalk ; 14th Light Dragoons, Longford ; 15th Hussars, Dublin ; 3rd Battalion Grenadier Guards, Dublin ; 1st Foot, 1st Battalion, Londonderry ; * 2nd Battalion, Athlone ; 7th, Drogheda ; * 9th, Youghal ; * 14th, Mullingar ; 18th, Limerick ; 24th, Kinsale ; * 25th, Armagh ; * 27th, Dublin ; 29th, Kinsale ; * 30th, Clonmel ; * 43rd, Cork ; 46th, Dublin ; 47th Foot, Boyle ; * 52nd, Enniskillen ; 56th, Cork ; * 60th, Nenagh ; 2nd Battalion, Kilkenny ; 67th, Cashel ; * 69th, Clare Castle ; * 70th, Cork ; * 74th, Belfast ; 76th, Boyle ; * 81st, Dublin ; 82nd, Belfast ; 83rd, Newry ; 85th, Galway ; 89th, Fermoy ; 90th, Naas ; 91st, Birr ; 94th, Cork ; 95th, Templemore ; 96th, Kinsale. Here is an array of bayonets that renders it difficult to believe that Ireland is other than a recently-conquered territory, throughout which an enemy's army has just distributed its encampments. Four times as many soldiers as comprise the standing army of the United States are at this time quartered in Ireland !

the immediate descendants of Irish. The quarter in which they congregate is, like the district of St. Giles's of London, a nursery of all the customs that belong to savage life. In the very centre of our otherwise civilised and wealthy town, a colony which has acquired for its *locale* the title of Little Ireland, exhibits all the filth, depravity, and barbarism that disgrace its patronymic land. Nor is the evil confined within such limits. Its influences are felt in the adulteration of character, and the lowering of the standard of living of our artisans generally : it is a moral cancer, that, in spite of the efforts of science or philanthropy to arrest its progress, continues to spread throughout the entire mass of our labouring population.

No part of England or Scotland is exempt from its share in the natural consequences of this terrible state of degradation to which the people of Ireland are reduced. There is not a village or parish of the kingdom into which its famine-impelled natives do not, at certain periods of the year, penetrate to share the scanty wages of our peasantry ; thus dragging them down to their own level, and, in return, imparting to them the sad secrets of their own depraved modes of life.

But great as this evil has hitherto been, it is only a subject of astonishment to us, that the immigration of the Irish people into this portion of the empire has not been more extensive : sure we are, from the accounts we have of the present state of the southern portion of that island, that nothing short of Berkley's wall of brass can for the future save us from an overwhelming influx of its natives.

Let those who are incredulous of our opinion consult the recent work on Ireland, from which we are about to offer an extract or two for the perusal of our readers.

We look upon every writer who directs the attention of the people of England to the *facts* connected with the present state of Ireland as a benefactor of his country. Even should an author, for the sake of being read, or for party purposes, like

Cobbett, throw some exaggeration into his pictures of the horrors of this land, we still view him in the useful capacity of a watchman, sounding the alarm of danger, scarcely too loud, to the indifferent minds of Great Britain. Though, like the hydro-oxygen microscope, when applied to physical objects, his descriptions magnify its social monsters, till their magnitude terrifies the beholder—still the monsters are there : they are only enlarged, and not created. In the purer elements of English society, such evils could not, through whatever exaggerating medium, be discovered.

But the traveller from whom we are about to quote gives intrinsic evidences of not only competent intelligence but strict impartiality and a sincere love of truth. We do not think that he possesses in an eminent degree the organ of causality, as the phrenologists call it; for he attributes as the ultimate cause of the miseries of Ireland the want of employment for its people, not recollecting that this evil must have its cause; but in the qualities of a careful and experienced observer of facts he is unquestionably a competent authority.

These are his words in speaking of the remuneration of labour in Ireland :—"I am quite confident that if the whole yearly earnings of the labourers of Ireland were divided by the whole number of labourers, the result would be under this sum—fourpence a day for the labourers of Ireland."

Again, in speaking of the habitations of the peasantry of Ireland, the following is the description given by the same author :—"The only difference between the best and the worst of the mud cabins is that some are water-tight, and some are not ; air-tight, I saw none ; with windows, scarcely any; with chimneys—that is, with a hole in the roof for the smoke to escape through—as many perhaps with it as without it. As for furniture, there is no such thing; unless a broken stool or two and an iron pot can be called furniture. I should say that in the greater part of Leinster and Munster, and in the flat districts of Connaught, bedsteads are far from general, and bed-clothing is never sufficient."

Let us reflect for a moment on what would be the effects upon the condition of our industrious population, if they were brought down to share one common average with these labourers ; a fate which, we repeat, they are doomed to suffer, unless by imparting peace and prosperity to Ireland, we shall succeed in elevating her people to our own level.

This intelligent traveller sums up his recital of all that he witnessed during a tour of many months throughout the island (great part of which time he spent in unrestrained intercourse with the peasantry), in these words, which, along with every other portion of his volumes, do equal honour to his moral courage and philanthropy :—

"I, Henry David Inglis, acting under no superior orders, holding no government commission ; with no end to serve, and no party to please ; hoping for no patronage, and fearing no censure ; and with no other view than the establishment of truth—having just completed a journey throughout Ireland, and having minutely examined and inquired into the condition of the people of that country—do humbly report that the destitute, infirm, and aged form a large body of the population of the cities, towns, and villages of Ireland : that, in the judgment of those best qualified to know the truth, three-fourth parts of their number die through the effects of destitution, either by the decay of nature accelerated, or through disease induced by scanty and unwholesome food, or else by the attacks of epidemics, rendered more fatal from the same causes : that the present condition of this large class is shocking for humanity to contemplate, and beyond the efforts of private beneficence to relieve, and is a reproach to any civilised and Christian country."

A Christian country does he say ? Posterity will doubt it ! There is no such picture as this of a permanent state of national existence to be found in any authentic history, ancient or modern, Christian or pagan. We shall search the volumes of the most accredited travellers in Russia,* Turkey,† or India, and find no description of a people that is not enviable, in comparison with the state of millions of our fellow-subjects in Ireland. The natives of Moldavia and Wallachia, which provinces have been the battle-fields for Turks and Christians for centuries, are now living in happiness and plenty, when compared with the fate of the inhabitants of a country that has known no other invader but England.

We lavish our sympathies upon the serfs of Poland, and the slaves of Turkey; but who would not prefer to be one of these, to the perishing with hunger under the name of freeman ? We send forth our missionaries to convert the heathen; but well might the followers of Mahomet or Zoroaster instruct us in the ways of charity to our poor Christian brethren !

Far be it from us to say, with a celebrated French writer, that we distrust the philanthropy of all those who seek in distant regions for objects of their charity ; but we put it to our countrymen, whether, in lending themselves to any scheme, having benevolence for remote nations in view, whilst such a case as this stands appealing at their doors, they are not, in the emphatic words of Scripture, " taking the children's meat and casting it to the dogs."

We shall be told that the hundreds of thousands of pounds that are sent annually to remote regions are for the promotion

* Dr. Clarke tells us that the serfs of Russia, when old, are of right supported by the owners of the estate.

† In the Koran, the charities are enjoined : and Tournefort tells us—"There are no beggars to be seen in Turkey, because they take care to prevent the unfortunate from falling into such necessities. They visit the prisons to discharge those who are arrested for debt ; they are very careful to relieve persons who are bashfully ashamed of their poverty. How many families may one find who have been ruined by fires, and are restored by charities ! They need only present themselves at the doors of the mosques. They also go to their houses to comfort the afflicted. The diseased, and they who have the pestilence, are succoured by their neighbours' purse."—*Vol. ii.*, p. 59. .The Bible still more strictly commands charity, and—see *Inglis' Ireland !*

of religion. But there cannot be religion where there is not morality ; and can morals survive in a starving community such as exists in Ireland? No! and, therefore, we say, until the above proclamation of her desperate sufferings be controverted (and who will gainsay it?) a copy of it ought to be affixed to every public building, and to the doors of every church and chapel in particular of England ; and all attempts, of whatever description, to subsidise the charity of this country, in behalf of alien nations, whilst this member of our own family, in the extremity of want, supplicates for succour at our hands, should be denounced and put aside by the common sense and humanity of the nation.

If not, if for more fanciful, because more distant, projects of benevolence, we neglect our obvious duty towards these our fellow-countrymen, then will the sins and omissions of their fathers be visited upon the future generations of Englishmen ; for assuredly will the accumulated ills of Ireland recoil upon their heads, until one common measure of suffering shall have been meted out to both !

But we will not forget that our object in entering upon the consideration of this subject was to illustrate the impolicy and injustice of the statesmen of this country, who have averted their faces from this diseased member of our body-politic ; and, at the same time, have led us, thus maimed, into the midst of every conflict that has occurred upon the whole continent of Europe. To give one example, let us only recur to the year 1823, when the French invasion of Spain drew forth those well-known powerful appeals of Brougham * to the ever-ready-

* In alluding to this eminent, and we fervently believe disinterestedly patriotic, individual, we have no wish to be thought to have caught the contagion of that virulence with which, perhaps from the unworthiest of motives, his character has been latterly assailed. We feel no very great respect for mere eloquence, which, from the time of Demosthenes down to that of the subject of these remarks, has, probably, as often been sacrificed at the altar of falsehood as upon the purer shrine of truth. But Lord Brougham's labours on behalf of popular intelligence, at a time, too, be it always remembered, when the cause of educa-

primed pugnacity of his countrymen, in which he exhausted
his eloquence in the cause of war against France; declaring,
amongst similar flights, that we ought to spend our last shilling
in behalf of Spanish independence; whilst at the very same
moment of time famine, pestilence, and insurrection were raging,
even to an unparalleled extent, in Ireland, whose natives were
driven to subsist on the weeds of the fields, and for whom a
subscription fund amounting to more than a quarter of a
million was that very year raised by the people of Great Britain.

tion was not, as now, fashionable, places his fame on a monument that is
based securely upon the broad and durable interests of the people.

At the very instant of penning this note, we have seen the report of a speech
made by Lord Brougham in the House of Lords upon the subject of foreign
politics, from which we subjoin an extract, illustrating how little the judgment
of this nobleman has profited by the interval since 1823 upon a question on
which, unluckily for England, her statesmen have, one and all, been alike
infatuated :—" With regard to the change of the sovereign in Austria, he could
not avoid expressing his hope that His Majesty's Government would seize upon
the opportunity offered by the change of the reigning Sovereign there, and
enforce, what *he knew their predecessors had tried to enforce* (!), the humane,
and in his conscience he believed the sound, prudent, and politic course, as
regarded the individual interest of the Austrian government, imposed upon the
government of His Imperial Majesty, to mitigate the rigours, if not to terminate
the sufferings, that, for nearly the whole of the last seventeen years, had been
inflicted upon some of the ablest, most accomplished, virtuous, and enlightened
individuals, the ornaments of the nobility of a part of His Imperial Majesty's
dominions. He hoped that an occasion would be taken of enforcing this subject on the attention of the Austrian government, in a manner that became the
character, the policy, and the *wisdom* (!) of this country ; for he was convinced,"
&c.—*Morning Chronicle Report, March 11th*, 1835.

The circumstances under which the above was uttered were even still more
inopportune than those we alluded to of 1823.

Under the same roof—at the very same instant of time in which an interference
with the domestic concerns of a capital nearly a thousand miles distant, and
with which we have scarcely more interested connection than with Timbuctoo, was
thus invoked—a debate was proceeding in the House of Commons (the malt
question), in which it was stated, by several speakers, that three-fourths of the
population of this kingdom are plunged in distress and poverty ; and in the
course of which the Chancellor of the Exchequer declared that he possessed
not the power of alleviating such misery ; whilst such was the extremity to
which this minister of the crown was driven, that he felt impelled to appeal to
the honesty of a British Parliament in behalf of the national creditor.

Subsequently, as our readers know, our Government des-
patched an armament to the succour of Portugal. We witnessed
the departure of those troops from London, and well do we
remember the enthusiasm of the good citizens on that occasion.
In the next meeting of Parliament it was stated that this display
of our power and magnanimity towards an old ally cost upwards
of a million sterling. Here was a sum that would have sufficed
to employ the starving peasantry of Ireland in constructing a
railroad fifty miles in length. What fruits have we to exhibit,
in the present state of the Peninsula, that can be said to have
grown out of this expenditure?

But the worst effects of an intermeddling policy are, that
we are induced at all times to maintain an *attitude*, as it is
termed, sufficiently formidable, in the face of Europe. Thus,
the navy—which, after the peace was very properly reduced,
so that in 1817 it comprised only 13,000 seamen and 6,000
marines—was, under the plea of the disturbed state of
Europe, from time to time augmented; until, in 1831, the
estimate amounted to 22,000 seamen and 10,000 marines;
whilst the army, which in 1817 had been cut down to 69,000
men, was, by successive augmentations, raised to 88,000 men
in 1831.

Our limits do not allow us to go further into details upon
this portion of our task. But we cannot dismiss the subject
altogether without a few observations upon the remedies which
are proposed for the present state of Ireland. That "every
quack has his nostrum for the cure of poor Erin," is a common
remark with her people; and although we find the doctors, as
usual, differ exceedingly in opinion, there are two prescriptions
which have been very numerously recommended—we allude to
a law against absenteeism, and a poor law.

We should hail any measure that promised the slightest
relief to the wretched people of this country. But it is necessary to ask, Could these plans, through any law, be efficaciously
enforced? There is, we think much raving after impracticable

legislation nowadays. Let us see if these be not specimens of it.

We never yet met with a person who professed to under-stand how an Act of Parliament could be framed, that, without committing the most grievous injustice and cruelty, would be more than a dead letter against Irish absenteeism. Let us imagine that a law was enacted to compel every owner of an estate in Ireland to reside upon his property. Well, this would be imprisonment for life. No, is the answer : he might range over the whole island, and even reside on the sea-coast, or, for a portion of the year, in Dublin. Good: then he must have a passport, and at every move his person must be cog-nised ; and for this purpose a police, similar to the French gensdarmerie, must be organised throughout the country. But the traders, the farmers, the professional men, the tourists, the beggars, the commercial travellers, the strangers—all these, we suppose, would be subjected to the like *surveillance ?* Oh, no ! must be the reply : that would be to obstruct the entire business of the country. Thus this law falls to the ground, since the landowner might elude it under any of these disguises.

But to approach the subject in another way. The enact-ment would not, of course, be passed without some clauses of exceptions. It would be barbarous, for example, to prohibit a man from changing his abode, if illness demanded it, or if his wife or children were in that extremity. What, then, would be the market price of a doctor's certificate, to transport a *malade imaginaire* to France or Italy? Again, if a Milesian landlord pined for a trip to London, would not a subpœna to attend some law process be a favourite resource ? Or a friend might summon him before a parliamentary committee, or find him comfortable apartments in the rules of the Fleet. Fictitious conveyances, nominal divisions of property, and a thousand other expedients, might be named, for rendering nugatory this law, each one of which would, to a reasonable mind, prove the impracticability of such a measure.

Let those who think that a poor's rate, sufficient to operate as a relief to the pauper population, could be levied in the south of Ireland, peruse Inglis's description of the present state of the province of Connaught. How would the rate be agreed upon, when no one of the wretched farmers would come forward to fix the amount? Or, if they did agree to a levy, who would be bold enough to collect the rate? Who would distribute it, where all are needy of its assistance? But, for the sake of contemplating the probable effects of such a law, let us suppose that these difficulties were got over. We believe that those who recommend a poor law as a remedy for Ireland are imperfectly acquainted with its desperate condition.

The poor's rate of England had, two years ago, in various districts, reached fourteen shillings in the pound ; and, in one instance, it absorbed the entire rental of the land ; and this occurred in Buckinghamshire, within fifty miles of London, and where there are rich farmers and landowners.

What, then, would be the effects of any poor law in a country where parish after parish, throughout vast districts, contains not an inhabitant who tastes better food than potatoes, or knows the luxury of shoes and stockings, or other shelter than a mud cabin? We dread to contemplate the results which, in our judgment, would follow such an attempt to ameliorate the lot of this population. As soon as a competent provision for the poor were ordered—such as a Christian legislature must assign, if it touch the subject at all—the starving peasantry of Ireland, diverted from their present desperate resources of emigration or partial employment in towns, would press upon the occupiers of the soil for sub-sistence, with such overwhelming claims as to absorb the whole rental in less than six months. What must follow, but that every person owning a head of cattle or a piece of furni-ture, would fly to the cities ; leaving the land to become a scramble to the pauper population, which, in turn, abandoned to its own passions, and restrained by no laws or government, would probably divide itself once more into septs, under separate chieftains (the elements of this savage state are still in existence in many parts of the south of Ireland), and commence a war of extermination with each other. The days of the Pale and all its horrors would be again revived ; famine would soon, of necessity, ensue ; the towns would be assailed by these barbarous and starving clans ; and the British Government would once more be called on to quell this state of rapine with the sword.

Such, we conscientiously believe, would be the inevitable consequences of a measure which, to the eye of the uninformed or unreflecting philanthropist, appears to be the most eligible plan for the peace and prosperity of Ireland.

What remedies, then, remain for this suffering country ?

We shall pass by the cry for the repeal of the Union ; because everybody knows that to have been only used as an engine for the purpose of acquiring a power to coerce England into other acts of justice. A Parliament in Dublin would not remedy the ills of Ireland. That has been tried, and found unsuccessful ; for all may learn in her history that a more corrupt, base, and selfish public body than the domestic legislature of Ireland never existed ; and the very first declaration of the United Volunteers, when, in 1781, they took the redress of her thousand wrongs into their own hands, was to the effect, that they resolved to use every effort to extirpate the corruptions that so notoriously existed in the Irish Parliament ; and one of the first acts of the same patriotic body was to invest the Parliament House in Dublin, and at the point of the bayonet, to extort from those native legislators a redress of their country's grievances.

To come, next, to the scheme of emigration. All must regard with feelings of suspicion and disfavour any attempt to expatriate a large body of our fellow-countrymen ; and we hold such an antidote to be only like removing the slough which has arisen from a wound, whilst the disease itself remains untouched.

But, unhappily, the maladies of Ireland have taken such deep root, that legislation cannot hope, for ages to come, effectually to eradicate them; whilst here is a mode by which hundreds of thousands 'of our fellow-creatures are eager to be enabled to escape a lingering death. Surely, under such circumstances, this plan, which would leave us room to administer more effectually to the cure of her social disorders, deserves the anxious consideration of our legislature.

Here let us demand why some forty or fifty of our frigates and sloops of war, which are now at a time of peace sunning themselves in the Archipelago, or anchoring in friendly ports, or rotting in ordinary in our own harbours, should not be employed by the Government in conveying these emigrants to Canada, or some other hospitable destination? The expense of transporting an individual from Limerick to the shores of America by such a method would probably not exceed two pounds. On arrival the Government agents might probably find it necessary to be at the charge of his subsistence for a considerable time—perhaps not less than twelve months.

Altogether, however, the expense of a project of emigration, on a scale of magnitude, must be enormous. But, again, we say that any present sacrifice on the part of the people of this country, by which the Irish nation can be lifted from its state of degradation, will prove an eventual gain.

Contemporary with any plan of emigration, other projects for the future amelioration of the fate of that miserable people must be entered upon by the British Parliament; and we should strongly advocate any measure of internal improvement which, by giving more ready access to the southern portion of the island, would throw open its semi-barbarous region to the curiosity and enterprise of England. Steam navigation has already given a powerful stimulus to the industry of the eastern maritime counties; and if, by means of railroads, the same all powerful agent could be carried into the centre of the kingdom, there can be no doubt that English capital and civilisation would follow in its train. Every one conversant with the subject is aware how greatly the pacification and prosperity of the Scotch Highlands were promoted by carrying roads into these savage districts ; and still more recently, how, by means of the steam navigation of the lakes, and the consequent influx of visitors, the people have been enriched and civilised. Similar effects would doubtless follow, if the facilities of railroad travelling were offered to Ireland, whose scenery, hardly rivalled in Europe, together with the frank and hilarious temperament of its people, could not fail to become popular and attractive with the English traveller.

We will here introduce a scheme to the notice of our readers which, whilst we gladly acknowledge with gratitude the source from whence it originated, we think deserves the notice of our Government.

In the *New York Courier and Enquirer* newspaper of December 24, 1834, appeared a letter headed "Traverse Atlantic," which, after stating that the writer, on a recent visit to Europe, had suffered a delay of ten days in ascending the French Channel, from Finisterre to Havre, and of eight days in descending the Irish Channel, from Liverpool to Cape Clear, says, he "believes that on an average one-third or one-fourth of the time is wasted upon every Trans-Atlantic voyage in getting into, or out of, the European ports now resorted to." The writer then proceeds as follows :—

"The commerce of America chiefly centres in the ports of Hamburgh, Havre, London, and Liverpool. Each of these is distant from the ocean and difficult of access. On the western coast of Ireland there are several harbours far superior in every requisite. As, for instance, the island of Valentia, which is the nearest point of land in Europe to America. Between it and the main reposes an excellent receptacle for shipping of any burden, approached by two easily practicable inlets, completely landlocked, capacious, and safe. Situated immediately on the brim of the Atlantic, a perfectly straight line can be drawn from this harbour to the port of New York, the intervening transit unobstructed by islands, rocks, or shoals. The distance being less than two thousand seven hundred miles may be traversed by steam in about eight days ; and the well-known enterprise of the American merchants renders it unnecessary for me to do more than to intimate that they will avail themselves of every opening or inducement that may arise to establish the first link of intercourse by a line of packet boats. * * * *

" The extent of this undertaking has been stated as beyond the means of those likely to engage in it. This seems to me incredible, when I advert to the facts that Ireland has a population of eight millions, multitudes of whom are in beggary for want of work, with wages at from fourpence to one shilling a day, and money, on the average, not worth more than three per cent. ; and recollect, at the same time, that the State of South Carolina, one of the smallest in the American Confederation, with a population of three hundred thousand, wages at five shillings sterling a day, and capital at seven per cent. interest, has, unaided, and by private enterprise, constructed a railroad from Charleston to Augusta, one hundred and forty-five miles in extent, at present the longest in the world, which is travelled by locomotive engines in the course of ten hours.

"The advantages to accrue to Ireland in particular by thus opening a regular communication from New York to London in twelve, and to Paris in fifteen days, are incalculable. That island would become, of necessity, the thoroughfare between the two hemispheres : and the occupation of the public mind in such an enterprise, and the constantly increasing fruits of its progress, would do more to pacify the fearful dissensions of the people, and ameliorate their most lamentable condition, than any legislation of even the best disposed Parliament."

The above project, which, in the affluence of their enterprise, our American friends have suggested for the benefit of

Ireland, merits the attention of the landowners and patriots concerned for the welfare of her people.

It has long been decided by the merchants and nautical, men engaged in the intercourse between Liverpool and America, that steamboats* would be found capable of navigating the Atlantic with perfect safety ; and the more sanguine amongst those interested in increasing the facilities of communication between the two countries have gone so far as to predict that, in a dozen years' time, we may hope to witness the arrival and departure of steamers twice a week between England and the United States.

As any scheme of this nature must necessarily require that the vessels should take their departure from the nearest points of approximation of the two hemispheres, Ireland would thus become the starting-place for all Europe ; and it is scarcely possible to conceive anything that would be more calculated to enrich and civilise that country than by thus irrigating it, as it were, with the constant tide of emigration to and from America.†

A railway, for the purpose here alluded to, would pass through the centres of Leinster and Munster, intersecting the counties of Kildare, Queen's County, Tipperary, Kilkenny, Limerick, Cork, and Kerry ; and would pass within twenty miles of the port of Limerick, and thirty miles from that of Cork, to both of which cities, it might reasonably be expected, that branches would be carried by public subscription : thus, not only would these two great commercial havens be connected with Dublin, but by opening a direct communication with each other, it would afford a medium for traffic, by steam, between the fifteen counties that are washed by that noble

* In June, 1819, a steamship crossed the Atlantic from Savannah to Liverpool.

† [In 1858, when the Earl of Eglinton was Lord Lieutenant, the first Irish Trans-Atlantic packet station was established at Galway ; and in about a year later Cork was made a port of call for the Inman steamships, and subsequently for the Cunard line.]

stream, the Shannon, and the ports of Cork and Bristol; and, ultimately, by means of the Great Western Railway, with London.

Railroads are already begun for connecting Liverpool with Southampton, by way of Birmingham and London. The French have long been engaged in making surveys for a railway from Havre, by way of Rouen (the Manchester of France), to Paris; and although characteristic delays may arise to retard the completion of this, as of other projects of mere usefulness, with that fanciful people, yet, as it is, perhaps, the only line in all France that would prove a remunerating speculation, there can be no doubt that it will be the first that is undertaken in that country.

Presuming this to be effected, then, by means of such a plan as is here recommended, for constructing a line from Dublin to the extreme point of Munster, a traveller would be enabled to transport himself from the French metropolis, *viâ* Havre, Southampton, London, Liverpool, and Dublin, to Valencia Island, or any other point of embarkation on that coast, in about sixty hours; and, as the voyage to New York would be accomplished in about eleven or twelve days, the whole distance from Paris to America, which now, upon an average, occupies forty days in the passage, would be accomplished, by the agency of steam, in about a third of that time.

That such a project, if completed, would secure the preference of voyagers to all parts of North America, not only from Britain, but from every quarter of Europe, must be apparent; that all we have recommended is perfectly practicable we have no difficulty in believing; and that a traffic, of such magnitude as is here contemplated, would have the effect of imparting wealth and civilisation to the country through which it passed, all experience proves to be unquestionable.

But it is not merely the future benefit that must accrue to Ireland, from the construction of a railroad through her provinces, that we should alone regard. The present support of her unemployed peasantry is another cogent motive for some such undertakings; for, unless a diversion of the surplus labour from the land be effected, through the employment of English capital amongst its population, no change can be attempted in the agricultural economy of Ireland. There is not, absolutely in the present densely crowded state of her rural inhabitants, elbow-room, so to speak, sufficient for readjusting their position. Yet there are reforms indispensably requisite to the agricultural prosperity of the island. The farming implements of its people are, for example, notoriously inferior, requiring twice the labour, both of men and cattle, of our own; yet, how shall we hope to see any improvements effected in these, by which the demand for labour shall be temporarily diminished, whilst one-half of the peasantry is perishing for want of work?

Again : the farms are so minutely subdivided, to meet the desperate competition of a people who possess no resource but the land to preserve them from famine, that their occupiers are destitute altogether of capital, and aim at no other end but to secure a daily subsistence on potatoes.

Under a better system, the cultivation of flax might be extended almost indefinitely. At present, the estimated value of the annual production of this raw material of their staple manufacture is about £1,500,000, which is yielded from one hundred thousand acres of land—not one-tenth of the area of a moderate-sized county.* But how can we apply a remedy to these, or the other evils of the soil, amidst a ferocious and lawless community, that visits with fire and sword † the prædial reformer?

We confess we see no hope for the eventual prosperity of

* [On June 21st, 1864, the Secretary for Ireland stated that in 1854 there were 151,403 acres under flax cultivation; in 1863, 214,063 acres; and in 1864 about 300,000 acres.]

† The barbarities committed in Ireland as frequently spring out of feuds arising from the competition after land as from disputes upon the question of tithes.

this country, except in the employment of a portion of its people, through the instrumentality of English capital, in the pursuit of manufactures or commerce. Of capital they are literally more destitute, in some parts of the west coast of the island, than are the North American Indians on the banks of the Mississippi ; as an instance in proof of which, it may be stated that, in a recent Government survey of that quarter, a vessel of war was the first to discover some of the finest fishing stations to be found in the British waters ; and yet the natives of the neighbouring shores possess not the means of procuring boats or nets, through which to avail themselves of these treasures !

Capital, like water, tends continually to a level ; and, if any great and unnatural inequality is found to exist in its distribution over the surface of a community, as is the case in this United Kingdom, the cause must, in all probability, be sought for in the errors or violence of a mistaken legislation. The dominant Church, *opposed to the national religion*, is, we conscientiously believe, in this case the primary existing cause of this discrepancy. Capitalists shrink, with all the susceptibility of the barometer in relation to the natural elements, from the storms and tempests of party passion; but how infinitely beyond all other motives must this privileged class be impelled, by the impulses of feeling and taste, to shun that atmosphere where the strife of religious discord rages with a fury unheard of in any other land !* There cannot be prosperity for Ireland, until the law, by equalising the temporalities of Catholics and

---

* When, at the commencement of the last century, a commission of the most intelligent merchants of Holland drew up, at the request of the Government, a statement of the causes of the commercial prosperity of that country, they placed the following words first in the list of "moral causes" :—"Among the moral and political causes are to be placed—The unalterable maxim and fundamental law relating to the free exercise of different religions ; and always to consider this toleration and connivance as the most effectual means to draw foreigners from adjacent countries to settle and reside here, and so become instrumental to the peopling of these provinces."

Protestants, shall have removed the foundation of this hideous contention.

To this consummation we must be ultimately driven; for nothing short of this will content the people of Ireland, because less would be short of the full measure of justice. We advocate no spoliation; let the vested rights of every individual be respected—especially let no part of the tithes fall to the merciless grasp of the landlords of Ireland, who, with many exceptions, may be regarded as the least deserving body of its people. But let the British Parliament assert the right to the absolute disposal of the Irish Church revenues, excepting in cases of private property; and let an equal government grant be applied to the religious instruction of both faiths, *according to the numbers of each*, as is the rule in France and Belgium* at the present day.

Such a regulation, by preventing Englishmen from holding benefices in Ireland (there would be no longer the temptations of rich livings and sinecures), would lead to a beneficial influence of the Protestant ministers in that country; for what could so much tend to destroy all hope of their proselyting the poor Catholics, what in fact could be so much calculated to make those ministers " despised and rejected," † as to send

* At the last sitting of the Belgian Chambers, a sum of £400 was voted towards the support of the English chapel; and a similar amount was granted for the service of the Jewish faith.

† " In planting of religion, thus much is needful to be done—that it be not sought forcibly to be impressed into them with terror and sharpe penalties, as now is the manner, but rather delivered and intimated with mildnesse and gentlenesse, *so as it may not be hated before it be understood, and their professors despised and rejected.* And therefore it is expedient, that some discreete ministers of their owne countrymen be first sent over amongst them, which, by their meeke persuasions and instructions, as also by their sober lives and conversations, may draw them first to understand, and afterwards to imbrace the doctrine of their salvation; for if that the auncient godly fathers which first converted them, when they were infidells, to the faith, were able to pull them from idolatry and paganisme to the true beliefe in Christ, as St. Patrick and St. Colomb, how much more easily shall godly teachers bring them to the true understanding of that which they already professed? Wherein is the great

amongst them, as is now the case, and ever has been, strangers, who, whatever may be their worth (and we believe the Church of England clergy, *as a class*, to be at this moment about the best body of men in Ireland), are ignorant of the character and habits, nay, even of the very language of the people? What chance have these in competition with the Roman Catholic priesthood, who, drawn from the middle or lower ranks of their countrymen, after an appropriate education in Maynooth College (where are always four or five hundred of such students), are sent back to, perhaps, their native village, to resume the personal and familiar acquaintance of its inhabitants?

Would the spiritual interests of the Scotch people be consulted by displacing their present excellent native pastors in favour of the younger sons of English noblemen?

If it be objected that the English Establishment is involved in the fate of the Church of Ireland, we answer, that the circumstances of the two are as opposite a complexion as light is to darkness. In England, the National Church comprises within its pale a great majority of the people: whilst in Ireland we behold a State religion upheld for the exclusive benefit of one-seventh of its population. Can we on the face of the earth find another example of an established church opposed to the consciences of six-sevenths of its supporters; for although the revenues may not go directly from their pockets, *could the*

wonder to see the oddes that is betweene the zeale of Popish priests and the ministers of the gospell ; for they spare not to come out of Spaine, from Rome, and from Remes, by long toyle and dangerous travayling hither, where they know perill of death awayteth them, and no reward or riches is to be found, only to draw the people unto the Church of Rome. Whereas some of our idle ministers, having a way for credite and estimation thereby opened unto them, and having the livings of the country offered unto them, without peines and without perile, will neither for the same nor any love of God nor zeale of religion, nor for all the good they may doe by winning soules to God, bee drawne foorth from their warme nestes to look out into God's harvest, which is even ready for the sickle and all the fields yellow long ago ; doubtless those good olde godly fathers will (I fear mee) rise up in the day of judgment to condemne them."—*Spenser.*

*present income of the Protestant Church be raised without the
Catholic population ?*

What should we say if the Government of Austria, Russia,
or Turkey (for each of these has a state religion, differing from
ours, and from one another, and yet pronounced by the law of
the land to be the only true belief), were found to be applying
the whole of the religious revenues of its country to the service
of the faith of one-seventh of its subjects? What should we
think if the Russian Government were to bestow the entire of
the property of the Greek Church upon the Catholic or
Armenian fraction of its people? In every country we find
the established religion in harmony with the cansciences of its
people, excepting in Ireland, which, in this, as in other
respects, presents to us an anomaly, which has no resemblance
amongst the nations of the world.

In concluding our observations upon this portion of our task,
we shall briefly ask—Does not the question of Ireland, in every
point of view, offer the strongest possible argument against the
national policy of this country, for the time during which we
have wasted our energies and squandered our wealth upon all the
nations of the Continent : whilst a part of our own Empire,
which, more than all the rest of Europe, has needed our attention, remains to this hour an appalling monument of our
neglect and misgovernment ? Add to this, that our efforts have
been directed towards the assistance of States for whose welfare
we are not responsible ; whilst our oppression and neglect have
fallen upon a people over whom we are endowed with the
power and accountable privileges of government—and the
extent of the injustice of our statesmen becomes fully dis-
closed.

The neglect of those duties which, in such a case devolve
upon the governor, as in the instance of every infringement of
moral obligations, bears within it the seeds of self-chastisement.
The spectacle of Ireland, operating like a cancer in the side of
England—of Poland, paralysing one arm of the giant that

oppresses her—of the two millions of negroes in the United States, whose future disposal baffles the ingenuity of those statesmen and philanthropists who would fain wash out this indelible stain upon their religion and government:—these are amongst the lessons which, if viewed properly, serve to teach mankind that no deed of guilt or oppression can be perpetrated with impunity even by the most powerful—that early or late, the invincible cause of truth will triumph against every assault of violence or injustice.

May the middle classes of Great Britain, in whom the government of this country is now vested, profit, in the case of Ireland, by these morals of past history!

Part III

AMERICA.

It is a singular fact that, whilst so much of the time and attention of our statesmen is devoted to the affairs of foreigners,
and whilst our debates in Parliament, and the columns of our
newspapers, are so frequently engrossed with the politics of
petty States, such as Portugal, Belgium, and Bavaria, little notice
is taken of the country that ought, beyond all others, to engage
the attention, and even to excite the apprehension of this commercial nation.

A considerable portion of our countrymen have not yet
reconciled themselves to the belief that the American colonies
of 1780 are now become a first-rate independent power.   The
more aged individuals of this party, embracing, of course, a
considerable section of the House of Peers, possess a feeling of
half pique and half contempt towards the United States, somewhat analogous to that which the old Scotch Jacobite lady
described by Burns indulged with reference to Great Britain
more than half a century after it had *rebelled*, as she persisted in
designating it, against the legitimate rule of the Stuarts.

We have met with persons of this very respectable and influential party who believe conscientiously that the Americans threw
off the yoke of the mother country, merely with a view to escape
the payment of certain sums of money due to English creditors ;*
and that they have ever since been struggling after a dubious
kind of subsistence by incurring fresh debts with us, and occa-
sionally repaying our credulity in no very creditable coin.   If

* " Who could their Sovereign, in their purse, forget,
  And break allegiance but to cancel debt."—*Moore.*

these be told that the people of the United States constitute our largest and most valuable commercial connection—
that the business we carry on with them is nearly twice as
extensive as with any other people, and that our transactions
are almost wholly conducted on ready money terms—they will
express surprise ; but then they will predict that no good will
arise ultimately from trading with Yankee Republicans.

If a word be said about the well-known religious and
moral character of the Americans, these worthy people with
stop you with the exclamation of, " How can there be religion
or morality in a country that maintains no established
church ? "

Offer to enter into an argument with these spirits of olden
time, or to adduce evidence in reference to the present condition of the American States, and ten to one, you will find
that they have read the works of no authors or travellers upon
that country, with the exception of those of Moore, Mrs.
Trollope, and Basil Hall. If the news-rooms and the libraries
that are under the direction of this prejudiced party be consulted, the former will be found to contain no specimens of the
millions of newspapers that issue, cheap as waste paper, from
the press of the United States : whilst, from the shelves of
the latter, all books * calculated to give a favourable picture
of the state of its flourishing community are scrupulously excluded.

Should we look into the periodical journals which are under
the patronage of the same class, we shall find the United States'

* An instance of this nature has come to our own knowledge. A gentleman
presented to the Lincoln Mechanics' Institution a copy of Stuart's work on
America (probably the best, because the most matter-of-fact and impartial of
all the writers upon that country), which an influential and wealthy individual
of the neighbourhood, one of the patrons of the society, induced the committee
to reject. We do not feel intolerant towards these errors of judgment, the
fruits of ignorance or a faulty education. The only wonder is, in this instance,
to find such a character so out of his element as to be supporting a Mechanics'
Institute at all !

news but rarely admitted to their columns, unless it be of a
nature that tends to depreciate the character of Republican
institutions, or serves as an occasion for quizzing the social
peculiarities of American society.

Yet it is to the industry, the economy, and peaceful
policy of America, and not to the growth of Russia, that our
statesmen and politicians, of whatever creed, ought to direct
their anxious study ; for it is by these, and not by the efforts of
barbarian force, that the power and greatness of England are in
danger of being superseded ; yes, by the successful rivalry of
America, shall we, in all probability, be placed second in the
rank of nations.

Nor shall we retard, but rather accelerate this fate, by closing
our ears, or shutting our eyes, to all that is passing in the
United States.   We regard it as the first duty of every British
statesman, who takes an enlightened interest in the permanent
grandeur of his country, however unpalatable the task may
prove, to weigh, in comparison with all the features of our
national policy, the proceedings in corresponding measures on
the other side of the Atlantic.   Possibly we may not, after all,
be enabled to cope with our more fortunate rivals in the energy
or wisdom of their commercial legislation, owing to the embarrassments and burdens with which we are encumbered ; but
still, it only the more becomes the character for high moral
courage that belongs to us to strive to understand from which
quarter danger is the most to be apprehended.

By danger we do not, of course, allude to warlike hostilities.
England and America are bound up together in peaceful fetters
by the strongest of all the ligatures that can bind two nations
to each other, viz., commercial interests ; and which, every
succeeding year, renders *more impossible*, if the term may be
used, a rupture between the two Governments.   This will be
sufficiently apparent when we state that a population of
upwards of a million of the inhabitants of this country,
supported by the various branches of the cotton industry,

dependent for the supply of the raw material upon the United States,* would be deprived of subsistence ; at the same time that a capital of thirty millions sterling would for the moment be annihilated—if such a catastrophe were to occur as the suspension of the commerce between England and the United States ; whilst the interests of the Americans would be scarcely less vitally affected by the same circumstance.

But we allude to the danger in which we are placed, by being overshadowed by the commercial and naval ascendancy of the United States. It has been through the peaceful victories of mercantile traffic, and not by the force of arms, that modern States have yielded to the supremacy of more successful nations. Thus the power and civilisation of maritime Italy succumbed to the enterprise of Spain and Portugal ; these again were superseded by the more industrious traders of Holland ; who, in their turn, sank into insignificance before the gigantic growth of the manufacturing industry of Great Britain ; and the latter power now sees, in America, a competitor in every respect calculated to contend with advantage for the sceptre of naval and commercial dominion.

Whether we view the rapid advance of the United States, during the last forty years, in respect of population or wealth, it is equally unparalleled in any other age or country. The past history, however, of this country is so well known, indeed, it is compressed into so short a space of recent history, that it would be trite to dwell upon it : our object is to draw a short comparison between the future prospects of the two countries.

The population of the United States was, at the first census, taken in 1790, found to be 3,929,328 ; and, in 1830, the number had, according to the fifth Government return, reached 12,856,171, exhibiting an increase, during the last ten years, of thirty-three per cent. ; that is, doubling itself in rather less

* The total amount of cotton worked up in this country in 1832 was 277,260,490 lbs., of which no less a proportion than 212,313,690 lbs, was imported from the United States,

than twenty-five years.* In 1831, the population of the British Islands amounted to 24,271,763, being an increase of about fourteen per cent. upon the enumeration for 1821.† Looking, therefore, to the present proportionate increase of the two countries, and *considering the relative circumstances of each*, it may be predicted that, in thirty years, the numbers of the two people will be about equal; and we further find that, at the same ratio of augmentation, and making no allowance for the probable increase of emigration from Europe, the population of the United States will, in seventy years from this time—that is, during the lifetime of individuals now arrived at maturity— exceed one hundred millions.

These circumstances demonstrate the rapid tendency towards a superiority, so far as numbers go; but we apprehend that, in respect to the comparison of our commercial prospects with those of America, the position of Great Britain does not, according to facts which we have to state, wear a more flattering aspect.

We find, by a table in the "American Almanack" for 1835, that the exports from the United States for the year ending the 25th September, 1833, amounted to 90,140,000 dollars, or about twenty millions sterling of our money.

The British exports for the same period were £47,000,000, of which thirty-six millions were of home commodities or manufactures, whilst the remaining eleven millions consisted of foreign and colonial produce. But it will be proper to exclude the colony trade from the question altogether, unless, in order to state the matter fairly, we agree to take into account, at the same time, the inhabitants of our dependencies, which would not improve our case.

Now, in order to institute a fair comparison between the respective trades of the two countries, it will be necessary to

* [According to the census of 1860, the population of the United States was 31,676,267.]

† [The population of the United Kingdom in 1861 was 29,346,834.]

bear in mind that, at the above period, the population of America was about fourteen millions, whilst that of the British empire may be reckoned to have been twenty-five and one-half millions.

We arrive, then, at this result, that, whilst our population, as compared with that of the United States, is as $25\frac{1}{2}$ to 14,* our commerce bears the proportion from 36 to 20. Further, if we compare the mercantile navy of Britain with that of America, we find the tonnage of the former, in 1832, to have been 2,261,860; whilst that of the latter, in 1833, amounted to 1,439,450 tons; by all which it appears clear that America is, in proportion to its population, at this moment, carrying on as extensive a commerce as England, or any other State in the world.

But we should take a very inadequate view of the comparative progress of the two nations, unless we glanced at other circumstances, which will effect very oppositely the career of England and the United States in their future race of commercial rivalry.

This Republican people presents the only example of past —as we believe it will prove of future—history, in which a nation has honourably discharged its public debt; and the greatest financial pressure its Government will in future have to contend against, singular as the fact may appear to us, is the difficulty of applying its surplus treasure impartially to the services of the separate States. The time is gone by, we believe, when people could be found to argue that a national debt is a national blessing.† Sure we are that, in our case, no person possessing sound reason will deny that we, who find it

* Bearing in mind that two millions of the American population are negroes, it makes the commerce decidedly in favour of the United States.

† Another fanciful theory upon the subject of the debt, invented, we believe, by Coleridge (it must have been by a *poet*, for the consolation of less ideal minds), has been lately promulgated. We are told that the country is none the worse off for the national debt, because it is all owing to Englishmen ; and that, therefore, it is only like drawing off the blood from one part of the body to

necessary to levy upwards of thirty millions annually upon the necessaries of life, must be burdened with grievous disadvantages, when brought into commercial competition with the untaxed labour of the inhabitants of America.

But it is not only the load of debt, heavy as that is, that we have to contend with; our oppressive public establishments are, throughout, modelled, *unnecessarily, we believe, for the service of the commonwealth*, upon a scale enormously disproportioned to those of our more economical rivals. We will pass by the whole of our civil expenditure, because we have not space for the detailed notice of its individual items; and we shall proceed to notice, as more connected with the design of this pamphlet, our army and navy, as compared with the military and naval forces of the United States.

We find, from a table in " Reuss's Statistics of the United States," that the number of seamen in the American mercantile navy is estimated at 86,000; whilst the States Government employs, in vessels of war, 6,000* men. The British merchant service, exclusive of the colonial registry, supports 140,000 sailors; and the number voted for the royal navy, in

inject it into another vein—*it is still all in the system.* We feel sorry to molest so comfortable an illusion.

But does it make no difference in what manner the *outlay* is invested—whether eight hundred millions of capital be sunk in the depths of the sea, or put out to good interest? Is there no difference between such a sum being thrown away, *destroyed, annihilated*, in devastating foreign countries, whilst the nation is called upon, out of its remaining capital, and with its gratuitous labour, to pay the interest—and the like amount being employed in making canals, railways, roads, bridges, drains, docks, &c.; planting trees, educating the people, or in any other way in which it *would return its own interest of capital?*

* We believe, almost incredible as the fact is even to ourselves, that the British naval *commissioned* officers exceed, by upwards of a thousand, the whole number of the men and officers of the American navy. A comment of a similar tenor, applied to the army of England, is to be found in a following page.

Yet we are in the twentieth year of peace, and every King's speech assures us of the friendly disposition of all foreign powers!

1833, was 27,000 men. Thus, then, we arrive at the unsatis-
factory result that, whilst in America the Government, as
compared with the merchant service, contains in the proportion
of hands rather less than one in fourteen, the number of men
employed in the royal navy of Britain, in comparison with the
quantity supported by the merchant service, is nearly in the
ratio of one to five.

The royal navy of England actually in commission at this
time (see the *United Service Magazine* for February) consists
of one hundred and forty-eight vessels of war, of which there
appear to be, according to the same authority, forty-six in the
different harbours of Great Britain, thirty-three in the Mediterranean, thirteen on the coast of Africa,* twenty-seven in the
West Indies, and the remainder in various other destina-
tions.

We find, in the *American Almanack* for 1835, the United
States navy given as twenty-one ships of war, of the following
descriptions:—One line-of-battle ship, three frigates, ten sloops,
seven schooners.†

It appears, then, that our royal navy contains, as nearly as
possible, seven times as many ships as are to be found in the
Government service of America.

Now, whatever objections may be urged with respect to

* Upon what principle of justice are the people of these realms subjected
to the whole expense of attempting to put down the slave trade? We say
attempting, because it is well known that the traffic is carried on as actively as
ever ; and, during the last year, the number of negroes conveyed away from the
shores of Africa has been estimated at twenty thousand. Here is a horrid
trade, which will entail a dismal reckoning, at the hands of Providence, upon
the future generations of those countries that encourage it ! But by what right,
by what credentials from on high, does England lay claim to the expensive and
vain office of keeping all mankind within the pale of honesty ?

† These statements refer to the ships in commission. Our navy comprises
about six hundred vessels of all sizes and in all conditions. The whole American
naval force consists of seventy ships. Yet Sir James Graham, when bringing
forward our navy estimates for 1833, actually made use of this comparison to
justify our force. So much for the *usefulness* of that which is called dexterity
in debate !

other branches of expenditure, against a comparison of our burdens with the corresponding economy on the other side of the Atlantic, we think no reasonable mind will deny that it is by reference to the commerce of a people alone that we can form a correct judgment of their policy, so far as the marine service is concerned, and judge of their ability to support permanently their naval establishments.

The disadvantageous nature of our position, in comparison with that of America, will be better understood, if we repeat in two words, as the substance of what we have proved from the foregoing figures, that, whilst the population, exports, tonnage, and mercantile seamen of Great Britain are not double those of the United States, our royal navy is about six times as great as the corresponding Government force of that country.

But, if we proceed to a comparison of the land forces, we shall find them to exhibit a yet more striking disproportion in the burdens of the two nations.

The entire military service of America comprises rather less than 7,000 men. In 1833, the Parliament of Great Britain voted 90,000 soldiers for the army of this country. Here, then, we perceive the odds are—still bearing in mind the population, &c., of the two countries—as nearly as possible six to one against us.

If we had the space, however, to allow of our entering into a comparison of details, we should find that the proportion of our officers greatly exceeds the above ratio. It will suffice to prove this, when we add, that the number of our commissioned officers alone, at this time, exceeds the entire amount of the army of the United States ; and of these we see, by the Army List for 1835, that 2,087 are field-officers of and above the rank of major !

To render the comparison of the respective burdens of the two people more simple and complete, we shall add their expenditure under these heads.

In the budget of 1833, the army and navy estimates of Great Britain were as follows :—

Army	. . . . . .	£7,006,496
Navy	. . . . . .	4,505,000
Ordnance	. . . . .	1,634,817

making a total of £13,146,313 for these warlike purposes.

In 1832, according to the *American Almanack* for 1835, the military service of the United States, including fortifications, arsenals, armouries, ordnance, internal improvements, &c., cost £1,134,589, whilst the navy estimate was for £817,100, making a total of £1,951,689.

Thus, it appears, that our gross expenditure, under the United States heads, is in the ratio of six and a-half to one, as compared with that of America—a country, be it repeated, whose population, trade, and registered tonnage are more than the half of our own—a country, too, whose public debt is cancelled, whilst ours amounts to nearly eight hundred millions !

But it will be said that our local position making it necessary to guard our shores with this demonstration of power, and our colonies calling for a vigilant protection, render unfair a comparison of this kingdom with the United States. We believe it might be shown that the dependencies of Great Britain are, at this moment, and in future are destined still more to be, the source of a considerable amount of taxation and pecuniary loss to the mother country ; and we trust that some abler pen will be applied to the elucidation ot this important question.

With respect to our proximity to the Continent, we recommend the experiment to be tried, whether that need necessarily embroil us in continental politics. Let us imagine that all our ambassadors and consuls were instructed to take no further share in the domestic concerns of European nations, but, throwing overboard the question of the balance of power —as we have long done that equally absurd bugbear of our ancestors, the balance of trade—to leave all those people to their own quarrels, and to devote their attention, exclusively, after the example of the Americans, to the *commercial interests* of their country. This might prevent our diplomatists displaying their address in finessing with Metternich or Pozzo di Borgo ; it might save the bones of our couriers, who now scour the continent of Europe, carrying despatches and protocols ; and it might enable us to dispense with the services of one half of the establishment at the Foreign Office. But will any one who understands the subject pretend to tell us that our trade would suffer by such a change ?

Or if we imagine that our army and navy were reduced one-half, in consequence of this improvement of our policy, does any person seriously apprehend that these islands would be in danger of being molested by any European power ? If such there be, let him recollect that the British Empire contains a population of twenty-five millions of free people, compressed within a space of little more than three hundred miles square— probably a denser crowd of human beings than was ever found upon a similar area ; and, further, let it be borne in mind, that railroads are now in progress for connecting one extremity of England with the other, in such a way, that not only any required force of men, but the entire munitions of war, may be transported, in twelve hours, from Lancashire or Yorkshire to the coast of Sussex or Kent—thus converting, as it were, the entire island into a fortified position of such wonderful strength that the genius of Vauban or Marlborough could not have conceived anything so formidable. Which is the power of the Continent that will make a descent upon a people placed in such an attitude ?

But supposing even that such a scheme should be contemplated, it will be owned, we suppose, that some preparation for so mighty a conquest would be necessary, which must afford us the necessary time for preparations of defence. No one will contend that a fleet and an army of sufficient magnitude to pounce upon England for its prey, could be conjured up on the scene, like the creations of harlequin's wand, without the spectators knowing, or caring to know, that the machinery for so grand a performance had been long in contrivance.

Besides, is it not apparent that henceforth the pressure of their own domestic affairs will engross the resources, and will impair the external power of all the Governments of Europe? *Reform Bills* will be demanded by their people, but they will not be obtained without bloodshed ; and all must foresee that the struggle between the antagonist principles of feudalism and constitutionalism is inevitable throughout the whole of the Continent.

But to recur to the subject of America. It might be said that the primary cause of all the prosperity and happiness of its people is to be found in the wisdom of that advice which we have prefixed for the motto of this pamphlet. Happily for that nation, this precept has been religiously obeyed ; for never have the political concerns of other States been suffered for one hour to divert the United States' Legislature from the pursuit of the just interests of its own people. The results may be seen, not only in unparalleled advances in wealth and civilisation at home, but in the fact we have just demonstrated, and which, we doubt not, will surprise most of our readers, that even the foreign commerce of this people is, in proportion to population, as great, or greater, than our own, notwithstanding our battles by land and by sea, and notwithstanding those expensive fruits of our victories, the colonies, that east, west, north, and south own our dominion !

It is a question of very considerable interest to us, whether America will continue her career as a manufacturing country, after the protective duties, which have professedly created her present cotton and other interests, shall have, in pursuance of the recent tariff law, been partially repealed.

It is the opinion of some writers, whose works are entitled to deference, that the United States cannot for centuries become our rivals in manufactures. They argue that, with an unlimited extent of unsettled territory to tempt the inhabitants to engage in the natural labour of agriculture, they will not be induced, unless for much higher wages than in England, to follow the more confined and irksome pursuits of the factory or workshop.

But does not the present industry of the population of the New England States tend to prove that there is a disposition, in the people of the older portions of this country, to settle down into the pursuits incident to towns at an advanced stage of society, and leave to agriculture the natives of the newer States ? We shall find that the exports from Boston comprise— among other articles of domestic manufacture equally unconnected with the system of factory labour—annually, about 3,500,000 pairs of boots and shoes, 600,000 bundles of paper, together with a large quantity of cordage, nails, furniture, &c.

We are inclined, however, to view the natives of the maritime portion of the Union, but particularly the inhabitants of the New England States, as eminently commercial in their tastes and characteristics ; and, as such—looking to the amount of capital at present embarked in their cotton manufacture, as well as to the circumstances of the raw material being the produce of their own soil, and bearing in mind the prodigious increase that is taking place in the numbers of their people— we profess to see no prospect of this our own staple industry being abandoned ; and, if not given up, we may expect, from the well-known and well-deserved panegyric paid by Burke to the enterprise of the New Englanders, in prosecuting the whale-fishing, that the competition on the part of such a people will be maintained with energy.

The capital employed in the various branches of the cotton manufacture in the United States is, according to a calculation for 1832, in " Reuss's Statistics of America," in amount about £11,000,000 ; and the consumption of raw cotton is estimated at 173,800 bales, or about one-fifth of all the growth of the country, and, as nearly as possible, a fifth of the quantity worked up, during the same year, in Great Britain.

The greater portion of all the products of this labour is consumed at home : the rest is exported in the shape principally of heavy calicoes, that have sustained a competition with our own fabrics in the Mediterranean and the East.

Some occasional shipments of low yarns have been made to this country ; but these transactions have not been of considerable magnitude.

Bearing in mind that the supply of the raw material of nearly one-half of our exports is derived from a country that threatens to eclipse us by its rival greatness, we cannot, whilst viewing the relative positions of England and the United States at this moment, refrain from recurring to the somewhat parallel cases of Holland and Great Britain, before the latter became a manufacturing State, when the Dutchman purchased the wool of this country, and sold it to us again in the form of cloth. Like as the latter nation became at a subsequent period, we are now overwhelmed with debts, contracted in wars, or the acquisition of colonies ; whilst America, free from all burdens, as we were at the former epoch, is prepared to take up, with far greater advantages, the fabrication of their own cotton as we did of our wool. The Americans possess a quicker mechanical genius than even ourselves (such, again, was the case with our ancestors, in comparison with the Dutch), as witness their patents, and the improvements for which we are indebted to individuals of that country in mechanics—such as spinning, engraving, &c. We gave additional speed to our ships, by improving upon the naval architecture of the Dutch ; and the similitude again applies to the superiority which, in comparison with the British models, the Americans have, for all the purposes of activity and economy, imparted to their vessels.

Such are some of the analogous features that warrant the comparison we have instituted ; but there are other circum-

stances of a totally novel character, affecting in opposite
degrees the destinies of these two great existing commercial
communities, which must not be lost sight of.

The internal improvement of a country is, undoubtedly, the
first and most important element of its growth in commerce
and civilisation. Hence our canals have been regarded by
Dupin as the primary material agents of the wealth of Great
Britain. But a new invention—the railway—has appeared in
the annals of locomotion, which bids fair to supersede all other
known modes of land transit ; and, by seizing at once, with all
the energy of a young and unprejudiced people, this greatest
discovery of the age, and planting, as it were, its fruits first
throughout the surface of their territory, the Americans have
made an important stride in the career of improvement, in
advance of every nation of Europe.

The railroads of America present a spectacle of commercial
enterprise, as well as of physical and moral triumph, more truly
astonishing, we consider, than was ever achieved in the same
period of time in any other country. Only in 1829 was the experiment first made, between Liverpool and Manchester, of
applying steam to the navigation of land, so to speak, by means
of iron railways, for the conveyance of passengers and merchandise : and now, in 1835, being less than seven years after
the trial was first made and proved successful, the United
States of America contain upwards of seventeen hundred
miles of railroads in progress of construction, and of which
no less than one thousand miles are complete and in actual
use.*

---

* "The railroads, which were partly finished, partly in progress, at the time
when I visited the United States, were as follow :—

	MILES.
Baltimore and Ohio (from Baltimore and Pittsburgh) .	250
Massachusetts (from Boston to Albany) . . .	200
Catskill to Ithaca (State of New York) . . .	167
Charleston to Hamburgh (South Carolina) . . .	135
Boston and Brattleboro' (Massachusetts and Vermont) .	114
Albany and New York	160

The enthusiasm with which this innovation upon the ancient and slower method of travelling was hailed in America—by instituting a newspaper expressly for its advocacy, and by the readiness of support which every new project of the kind encountered—evinced how well this shrewd people discovered at a glance the vast advantages that must accrue to whichever nation first effected so great a saving in that most precious ingredient of all useful commodities, time, as would be gained by the application of a discovery which trebled the speed, at

	MILES.
Columbia and Philadelphia (from Philadelphia to New York)	96
Lexington and Ohio (from Lexington to Cincinnati)	75
Camden and Amboy (New Jersey)	60
Baltimore and Susquehanna (Maryland)	48
Boston and Providence (Massachusetts and Rhode Island	43
Trenton and Philadelphia	30
Providence and Stonington	70
Baltimore and Washington	38
Holliday's Burgh and Johnstown (Pennsylvania)	37
Ithaca and Oswego (New York)	28
Hudson and Berkshire (New York and Massachusetts)	25
Boston and Lowell (Massachusetts)	24
Senectady and Saratoga (New York)	21½
Mohawk and Hudson (New York)	15
Lackawaxen (from Honesdale to Carbondale, Pennsylvania)	17
Frenchtown to Newcastle (Delaware and Maryland)	16
Philadelphia and Norristown (Pennsylvania)	15
Richmond and Chesterfield (Virginia)	12
Manch Chunk (Pennsylvania)	9
Haarlem (from New York to Haarlem)	8
Quincey (from Boston to Quincey)	6
New Orleans (from Lake Pontchartrain to Orleans)	5¼

The extent of the railroads forms an aggregate of one thousand seven hundred and fifty miles. Ten years hence this amount of miles will probably be doubled or trebled; so that scarcely any other roads will be used than those on which steam-carriages may travel."—*Arfwedson's Travels in* 1834. [Note to the Sixth Edition of "England, Ireland, and America."]

[It may be stated on the authority of Mr. Robert H. Berdell, President of the Erie Railway Company, that thirty-five thousand miles of railway are now in operation in the United States, and that nearly three thousand millions of dollars are invested in these gigantic enterprises.]

the same time reducing the money-cost, of the entire intercourse of the community.

Already are all the most populous districts in the United
States intersected by lines of railroads; whilst, amongst the
number of unfinished, but fast advancing undertakings, is a
work, now half completed, for connecting Baltimore on the
Chesapeake with the Ohio river at Wheeling, a distance of
more than two hundred and fifty miles.

Not content, however, with all that has been done, or is
still doing, a scheme is at present favourably agitated in the
public press of that country, that shall connect Washington
city with New Orleans, by a series of railways, which, with
those already in progress between New York and Washington,
will join the Atlantic at the mouth of the Hudson and the
Mexican Gulf; a project which, if completed, will enable a
traveller to visit New York from New Orleans in four days—a
transition of scene that may be better appreciated when it is
remembered that a person might pass in winter from the frozen
banks of the Hudson into the midst of the orange and sugar
regions of the Mississippi in about ninety hours ! Other plans,
of even a more gigantic character, are marked out as in con-
templation, upon the latest map published of the United
States*—plans that nothing but the prodigies already achieved
by this people prevent us from regarding as chimerical.

It demands not a moment's reflection to perceive the
immense advantages that must ensue from these improvements
to a country which, like America, contains within itself, though
scattered over so wide a surface, all the elements of agricultural
and manufacturing greatness. By subjecting this vast territory
to the dominion of steam, such an approximation of the whole
is attained, that the coals and iron of Pennsylvania, the lead of
Missouri, the cotton of Georgia, the sugar of Louisiana, and the
havens of New York and New England, will all be brought
into available connection with each other; in fact, by the

* By Amos Lay.

almost miraculous power of this agent, the entire American continent will, for all the purposes of commercial or social intercourse, be compressed into an area not larger than that of England, supposing the latter to possess only her canals.

Nothing more strongly illustrates the disadvantages under which an old country, like Great Britain, labours in competing with her younger rival, than to glance at the contrast in the progress of railroads in the two empires.

At the same time that, in the United States, almost every day beheld a new railway company incorporated, by some one of the State's legislatures, at the cost only of a few dollars, and nearly by acclamation, the British Parliament intercepted by its votes some of the most important projects that followed in the train of the Liverpool railroad.

The London and Birmingham company, after spending upwards of forty thousand pounds, in attempting to obtain for its undertaking the sanction of the Legislature, was unsuccessful in the House of Lords. The following characteristic questions are extracted from the evidence taken before the committee :—

" Do you know the name of Lady Hastings' place ?—How near to it does your line go ?—Taking the look-out of the principal rooms of the house, does it run in front of the principal rooms ?—How far from the house is the point where it becomes visible ?—That would be about a quarter of a mile ? —Could the engines be heard in the house at that distance ?— Is there any cutting or embankment there ?—Is it in sight of the house ?—Looking to the country, is it not possible that the line could be taken at a greater distance from the residence of Lady Hastings ?   *   *   *   *   *   *   *

" Was that to pass through Lords Derby and Sefton's land ? —Yes, they both consented. They threw us back the first year, and we lost such a line as we could never get again. Since which they have consented to the other line going through their property. * * * Supposing that line as easy for you as the present, was there any objection arising from going through anybody's park?"

The following question, put on the same occasion, by a peer to a shopkeeper, is one that probably would not have been asked by any other person but a hereditary legislator :—

" Can it be of any great importance whether the article goes there in five or six hours, or in an hour and a half?"

The Brighton and several other railways were abandoned, through dread of the expensive opposition that was threatened in Parliament; amongst which the Great Western line was successfully opposed by the landowners, seconded by the heads of Eton College, under the plea that it would tend to impair the character of the scholars! And a large party, headed by the Marquis of Chandos, actually met in public to celebrate, with drinking and rejoicing, the frustration of this grand improvement. Yet this nobleman has since had the offer of a voice in the cabinet council of the King : and, but that he is as honest as he most assuredly is unenlightened and prejudiced, he might now be one of the ministers of this commercial country !

But to recur to the consideration of affairs on the other side of the Atlantic. There is another peculiarity in the present attitude of the American people, as compared with our own, that is probably more calculated than all others to accelerate their progress towards a superior rank of civilisation and power. We allude to the universality of education in that country. One thirty-sixth portion of all public lands, of which there are hundreds of thousands of square miles unappropriated, is laid apart for the purposes of instruction. If knowledge be power, and if education give knowledge, then must the Americans inevitably become the most powerful people in the world.

Some writers have attempted to detract from this proud feature in the policy of the United States, by adducing, as examples, the backwoodsman and his family, and holding up their uncultivated minds, as well as their privation of Christian instruction, as proofs of the religious and moral abandonment of American society; forgetting that these frontier sections of the community are thinly spread over an inhospitable wilderness, where it must be acknowledged that no State provision for mental improvement could possibly embrace all their scattered members. When a man is placed at the distance of perhaps ten miles from his next neighbour, he is driven, as Dr. Johnson observes, to become his own carpenter, tailor, smith, and bricklayer; and it is from no fault in the laws, but owing to the like unavoidable nature of things, that the same solitary individual must also be left to act the part of teacher and pastor.

But, by referring to the last message of the Government of New York to the legislature of that State, which happens to be before us, we are able to exhibit to our readers, by a very brief quotation, the state of education in that most populous division of the Union.

"In the whole range of your duties," says this most enlightened address, "there is no subject in which the interests of the people are more deeply involved, or which calls for higher efforts of legislative wisdom, than the cause of education. The funds already provided by the State for the support of common schools is large, but not so ample as the exceedingly great importance of the object demands." After some other details, it goes on to say—" Eight hundred and thirty-five towns and wards (the whole number in the State) have made reports for the year 1833. There are nine thousand eight hundred and sixty-five school districts; the whole number of children, between the ages of five and sixteen years, in the State, was five hundred and thirty-four thousand and two; and the number instructed in the common schools in 1833 was five hundred and thirty-one thousand two hundred and forty. * * * The whole amount expended during the year 1833, on the common schools, cannot fall short of one million two hundred thousand dollars."*

Bearing in mind that this refers only to one State of the Union, containing rather less than two millions of inhabitants, could we imagine a more striking contrast to the above state-ment than in the fact that, during the corresponding session of the British Parliament, a sum of £20,000 was voted towards educating the people of England, whilst, in close juxtaposition to this, was a grant of £60,000 for the purpose of *partly* fur-nishing Buckingham Palace !†

The very genius of American legislation is opposed to ignorance in the people, as the most deadly enemy of good government.   Not only are direct measures, such as we have just quoted in the case of New York, taken to instruct the poor throughout the United States—not only are all newspapers and advertisements untaxed—but care is used, by excepting from fiscal burdens the humblest ingredients of the *materiel* of printing—such as paper, rags, type, &c.—to render knowledge as cheap and accessible as possible.

The newspaper press forms a distinguishing and rapidly improving feature in the economy of the United States.   In

* [Mr. Bright, in the speech which he delivered at Birmingham on the 13th December, 1865, said :—" I have just seen a report of a speech delivered last night by Mr. Watkin, who has recently returned from the United States. Speaking of education, he says that, taking the nine Northern States to contain ten millions and a half of people, he found there were 40,000 schools, and an average attendance of 2,133,000 children, the total cost of their education being 9,000,000 dols.   In the four Western States, with a population of 6,100,000, there are 37,000 schools, with an average attendance of nearly one million and a half scholars, at a cost of 1,250,000 dols.   Thus, in a population of sixteen millions, there are 77,000 schools, to which every poor child can go, at a cost of £2,000,000 a year.   He thought this highly to the credit of our American cousins, and I perfectly agree with him on that point."]

† [This was written before the date of the education movement, in which Mr. Cobden from an early period took a conspicuous part.   According to the last Report of the Committee of Council on Education, the sum of £8,087,296 1s. 11d. has been expended n Parliamentary grants from 1839 to 31st December, 1864.   " The expenditure rom Education grants," in the latter year, amounted to £655,041 11s. 5d.]

1834, according to the *American Almanack* for 1835, the aggregate of newspapers published under different titles in America was 1,265, of which ninety were daily journals; and the entire number of copies circulated during the year is estimated at ninety millions.*

In the British Islands three hundred and sixty-nine newspapers are published, of which seventeen only issue daily.† The annual sale of these is estimated at about thirty millions.

If, therefore, we compare the newspaper press of America and England together, allowing for the disproportion of inhabitants in the two countries, we shall be compelled to acknowledge that there is more than six times as much advertising and reading on the other side of the Atlantic as in Great Britain.

There are those who are fond of decrying newspaper reading. But we regard every scheme that is calculated to make mankind *think*—everything that, by detaching the mind from the present moment, and leading it to reflect on the past or future, rescues it from the dominion of mere sense—as calculated to exalt us in the scale of being ; and whether it be a newspaper or a volume that serves this end, the instrument is worthy of honour at the hands of enlightened philanthropists.

We know of nothing that would tend more to inform the people of England, and especially of Ireland, than removing the excise fetters from our press. Independently of the facilities to commerce, and the benefits which must ensue to temperance and morals generally, a free press would, by cooperating with a good government (and henceforth it is our

* [The census of 1860 states that 4,051 newspapers and periodicals were then published in the United States, of which 3,242 were political, the remainder being devoted to religion and literature. The annual aggregate circulation of copies was estimated at 927,951,548.]

† [From " Mitchell's Newspaper Directory " for 1865 it appears that 1,271 journals are now published in the United Kingdom, exclusive of 554 Reviews and Magazines. There are no trustworthy statistics of the circulation of these publications.]

own fault if we have a bad one), assist essentially the efforts of those who desire to reduce the expenditure of the State, and help us to dispense with that costly voucher of our ignorance, the standing army of this country.

We have thus hastily glanced at a few of the points of comparison to be found in the prospects of Great Britain and America at this moment. To what shall we liken the relative situations of these two great commercial and naval rivals ? We will venture on a simile.

Such of our readers as remember the London tradesman of thirty years ago, will be able to call to mind the powdered wig and queue, the precise shoes and buckles, and the unwrinkled silk hose and tight inexpressibles, that characterised the shop-keeper of the old school. Whenever this stately personage walked abroad on matters of trade, however pressing or important, he never forgot for a moment the dignified step of his forefathers ; whilst nothing gratified his self-complacency more than to take his gold-headed cane in hand, and leaving his own shop all the while, to visit his poorer neighbours, and to show his authority by inquiring into their affairs, settling their disputes, and compelling them to be honest, and to manage their establishments according to his plan. His business was conducted throughout upon the formal mode of his ancestors. His clerks, shopmen, and porters all had their appointed costumes ; and their intercourse with their chief, or with each other, was disciplined according to established laws of etiquette. Every one had his especial department of duty, and the line of demarcation at the counter was marked out and observed with all the punctilio of neighbouring but rival States. The shop of this trader of the old school retained all the peculiarities and inconveniences of former generations ; its windows displayed no gaudy wares to lure the vulgar passer-by, and the panes of glass, inserted in ponderous wooden frames, were exactly constructed after the ancestral pattern. Such were some of the solemn peculiarities of the last generation of tradesmen.

The present age produced a new school of traders, whose first innovation was to cast off the wig, and cashier the barber with his pomatum-box, by which step an hour was gained in the daily toilet. Their next change was to discard the shoes and the tight unmentionables—-whose complicated details of buckles and straps, and whose close adjustment occupied another half-hour—in favour of Wellingtons and pantaloons, which were whipped on in a trice, and gave freedom, though perhaps at the expense of dignity, to the personal movements during the day. Thus accoutred, these supple dealers whisked or flew, just as the momentary calls of business became more or less urgent; whilst so absorbed were they in their own interests, that they scarcely knew the names of their nearest neighbours, nor cared whether they lived peaceably or not, so long as they did not come to break their windows.

Nor did the spirit of innovation end here ; for the shops of this new race of dealers underwent as great a metamorphosis as their owners. Whilst the internal economy of these was re-formed with a view to give the utmost facility to the labour of the establishment, by dispensing with all forms, and tacitly agreeing even to suspend the ordinary deferences due to station, lest their observance might, however slightly, impede the business in hand—externally the windows, which were con-structed of plate glass, with elegant frames extending from the ground to the ceiling, were made to blaze with all the tempting finery of the day.

We all know the result that followed from this very unequal rivalry. One by one the ancient and quiet followers of the habits of their ancestors yielded before the active competition of their more alert neighbours. Some few of the less bigoted disciples of the old school adopted the new-light system, but all who tried to stem the stream were overwhelmed ; for with grief we add, that the very last of these very interesting specimens of olden time that survived, joining the two generations of London tradesmen, and whose shop used to gladden the soul of every

Tory pedestrian in Fleet Street, with its unreformed windows, has at length disappeared, having lately passed into the Gazette, that Schedule A of anti-reforming traders.

That which the shopkeeper of the present day is to him of the last age, such, comparing great things with small, is the commercial position of America as contrasted with that of Great Britain at the present moment. Our debt may be called the inexpressibles or tights, which incessantly restrain us from keeping up with the nimble pace of our pantalooned rivals. The square-toed shoes * and the polished buckles may be compared to the feudal laws and customs which, in competition with Wellington-booted brother Jonathan, impede the march of improvement and the enterprise of Englishmen. The powdered wig and queue we shall liken to our Church Establishment, which, although very ornamental and imposing in appearance, does yet engross a great share of the time and attention of our Parliament to adjust it properly,† all of which the legislature of our straight-haired competitor has been enabled to apply to the encouragement of a more prosperous trade. The untaxed newspapers of America, with their wide expanses of advertisements, contrasted ‡ with the stamped sheets of this country, are the new and old-light windows of the two generations of shop-

* There is scarcely a large town in England whose prosperity and improvement are not vitally affected by the operation of our laws of entail. In the vicinity of Manchester scarcely any freehold land can be bought ; Birmingham is almost wholly built upon leasehold land ; Wolverhampton has long been presenting a dilapidated aspect, in the best part of the town, in consequence of the property required for improvement being in the hands of the Church, and consequently inalienable. In many parts, manufactures are, from the like obstructing causes, prevented extending themselves over our coal-beds. The neighbourhood of Bullock Smithy might be instanced, for example.

† It would form an instructive summary to collect from our parliamentary history, for the last three hundred years, details of the time spent in the vain endeavour to make conscience square with Acts of Parliament.—See the debates in both Houses on Ireland in 1832 and 1833, for examples.

‡ It is not uncommon to find two thousand advertisements, principally of merchandise, contained in a single copy of a New York journal. We have counted no less than one hundred and seventy announcements in one column

keepers. The quickened gait of the trader of to-day, and the formal step of his predecessor, are the railways of the United States in competition with our turnpikes and canals. And to complete the simile, if we would see in the conduct of the two nations a resemblance to the contrast between the policy of the dealer of the old school, who delighted to meddle in the concerns of his neighbours, and that of the reformed trades-man, who rigidly confined his attention to the duties of his own counter—let us picture England, interfering with and managing the business of almost every State in Europe, Asia, and Africa, whilst America will form no connection with any one of them, excepting as customers.

What! shall we consign Old England, then, to ruin? Heaven forbid! Her people are made of tough materials, and he would be but a dastardly politician that despaired of them even yet. We say not, then, that this country will, like the antique establishment of the individual trader, perish at the feet of its more youthful and active competitor; but we fer-vently believe that our only chance of national prosperity lies in the timely remodelling of our system, so as to put it as nearly as possible upon an equality with the improved manage-ment of the Americans.

But let us not be misconstrued. We do not advocate republican institutions for this country. We believe the govern-ment of the United States to be at this moment the best in the world; but then the Americans are the best * people; and we

or compartment of the *New York Gazette.* Of course the crowded aspect of one of these sheets, in comparison with a London newspaper, is as different as is one of the latter in contrast with a Salisbury or any other provincial journal.

* We mean individually and nationally. As individuals, because, in our opinion, the people that are the best educated must, morally and religiously speaking, be the best. As a nation, because it is the only great community that has never waged war excepting in absolute self-defence—the only one which has never made a conquest of territory by force of arms (contrast the conduct of this government to the native Indians on the Mississippi, with our treatment of the aborigines on the Swan River); because it is the only nation

have a theory that the government of every State is always, excepting periods of actual change, that which is the best adapted to the circumstances and wants of its inhabitants.

But they who argue in favour of a republic, in lieu of a mixed monarchy, for Great Britain, are, we suspect, ignorant of the genius of their countrymen. Democracy forms no element in the materials of English character. An Englishman is, from his mother's womb, an aristocrat. Whatever rank or birth, whatever fortune, trade, or profession may be his fate, he is, or wishes or hopes to be, an aristocrat. The insatiable love of caste that in England, as in Hindostan, devours all hearts, is confined to no walks of society, but pervades every degree, from the highest to the lowest.* Of what conceivable use, then, would it be to strike down the lofty patricians that have descended to us from the days of the Normans and Plantagenets, if we of the middle class—who are more enslaved than any other to this passion—are prepared to lift up, from amongst ourselves, an aristocracy of mere wealth—not less austere, not less selfish—only less noble than that we had deposed. No ! whatever changes in the course of time education may and will effect, we do not believe that England, at this moment, contains even the germs of genuine republicanism.

We do not, then, advocate the adoption of democratic institutions for such a people. But the examples held forth to

whose government has never had occasion to employ the army to defend it against the people ; the only one which has never had one of its citizens convicted of treason ; and because it is the only country that has honourably discharged its public debt.

The slavery deformity was forcibly impressed upon this people in its infancy by the mother country. May the present generation outgrow the blemish.

* A diverting specimen of aristocracy in low life is to be found in an amusing little volume, called, "Mornings at Bow Street." A chimney-sweep, who had married the daughter of a costermonger, against the latter's consent, applied to the magistrate for a warrant to recover the person of his wife, who had been taken away from him by her father. The father did not object to the character of the husband, but protested against the connection as being "*so low.*"

us by the Americans, of strict economy, of peaceful non-inter-
ference, of universal education, and of other public improvements, may, and, indeed, must be emulated by the Government
of this country, if the people are to be allowed even the chance
of surviving a competition with that republican community.
If it be objected, that an economical government is incon-
sistent with the maintenance of the monarchical and aristocratic
institutions of this land, then we answer, let an unflinching
economy and retrenchment be enforced—*ruat cœlum !*

Of the many lessons of unsophisticated and practical wisdom
which have—as if in imitation of that arrangement of perpetual
decay and reproduction that characterises all things in material
nature—been sent back from the New World to instruct the
Old, there are none so calculated to benefit us—because there
are none so much needed — as those maxims of providence
and frugality to which Franklin first gave birth, and which,
gaining authority and strength from the successive advocacy
and practice of Washington, Jefferson, and now of Jackson,
have at length become identified with the spirit of the laws and
institutions of the United States.

An attempt has been made latterly by that class of our
writers * denominated Conservative, to deride this parsimony
of the Franklin school as unworthy of the American character.
But we are, at this present moment, writhing beneath the
chastisement due to our violations of the homely proverbs of
" Poor Richard ; " and it is only by returning within the sober
limits of our means, and rigidly husbanding our time and
resources, and by renouncing all idle pomp and luxury—it is
by these methods only, and not by advocating still further
outrages of the laws of prudence, that this nation can be
rescued from the all but irretrievable embarrassment into
which its own extravagance and folly have precipitated it.

The first, and, indeed, only certain step towards a diminution of our government expenditure, must be the adoption of

---

* Basil Hall's spending class.

that line of foreign policy which the Americans have clung to, with such wisdom and pertinacity, ever since they became a people.

If ever there was a territory that was marked out by the finger of God for the possession of a distinct nation, that country is ours ; whose boundary is the ocean, and within whose ramparts are to be found, in abundance, all the mineral and vegetable treasures requisite to make us a great commercial people. Discontented with these blessings, and disdaining the natural limits of our empire, in the insolence of our might, and without waiting for the assaults of envious enemies, we have sallied forth in search of conquest or rapine, and carried bloodshed into every quarter of the globe. The result proves, as it ever must, that we cannot violate the moral law with impunity. Great Britain is conscious that she is now suffering the slow but severe punishment inflicted at her own hands—she is crushed beneath a debt so enormous that nothing but her own mighty strength could have raised the burden that is oppressing her.

Again we say (and let us be excused the repetition of this advice, for we write with no other object but to enforce it), England cannot survive its financial embarrassment, except by renouncing that policy of intervention with the affairs of other States which has been the fruitful source of nearly all our wars.

We trust that this opinion will be generated throughout the population of this country, and that the same spirit will be reflected, through its representatives in Parliament, upon the Government.

In future, it will not be sufficient that no question concerning the State policy of other nations is allowed to occupy the attention of our legislature, unless it be first shown that our own honour or our interests are involved in its consideration—it will not be enough that our fleets and armies are not permitted to take a part in the contentions of other nations ; all this will not avail unless our diplomatists and foreign secretaries are jealously restrained from taking a share, either by treaties or protocols, according to the invariable wont of their predecessors, in the ever-varying squabbles of our continental neighbours. By this course of policy, and by this alone, we shall be enabled to reduce our army and navy more nearly to a level with the corresponding burdens of our American rivals.

May we be allowed, once more, to refute the objection which will be urged, that our numerous fleets are necessary to the defence of our commerce? Then, we ask, does any one deny that the persons of American merchants, or their vessels, are as safe in every quarter of the world as our own? We have seen to how great a proportion of our tonnage the American mercantile navy now amounts; we have seen how vast an export trade they carry on; and we have seen with how small a Government force all this is protected; may not an unanswerable argument, then, be found here, in favour of dispensing, henceforth, with a portion of our enormous naval and military establishments?

Hitherto, whenever a war has at any time been threatened between two or more European States, however remote or however insignificant, it has furnished a sufficient pretence for our statesmen to augment our armaments by sea and by land, in order to assume an imposing attitude, as it is termed—forgetting, all the while, that by maintaining a strict neutrality in these continental brawls, and by diligently pursuing our peaceful industry, whilst our neighbours were exhausting themselves in senseless wars, we might be growing in riches, in proportion as they became poorer; and, since it is by wealth after all that the world is governed, we should, in reality, be the less in danger from the powers on the Continent, the more they indulged in hostilities with each other.

It is a common error with our statesmen to estimate the strength of a nation—as, for instance, is the case at this moment, in their appreciation of the power of Russia, Prussia, or Austria—according to the magnitude of its armies and navies ; whereas these are the signs, and, indeed, the causes, of real poverty and weakness in a people.

" Our public debt is cancelled," said Mr. Benton, a speaker at the dinner lately held at Washington to celebrate the extinction of the American debt—" our public debt is cancelled ; and there is more strength in those words than in one hundred ships of the line ready for battle, or in a hundred thousand armed soldiers." And, to exemplify the truth of this sentiment, we have subsequently beheld this very people, with only a few schooners and frigates, and seven thousand troops, menacing the French Government, *steeped in debt*, at the head of its million of fighting men, and its three hundred vessels of war.

To remove, if possible, for ever the extravagant chimera that haunts the Government and the people of this country, of our being in danger from any possible combination of continental hostilities, let us suppose, for the sake of argument, that Russia were to invade Turkey—or that France were again to cross the Rhine, having first seized upon Holland and Belgium, and attack Prussia and Austria—or that the Spaniards should seize upon Portugal—or that the Austrian Government were to invade Naples or Sardinia—or, if such a supposition be possible, let us imagine these powers to be engaged in a battle-royal all together ; now, does any sober and reasoning mind believe that Great Britain, who, we will presume, had wisely availed herself of the opportunities afforded by her insular position to remain neuter, would be selected by any one of these powers, in addition to the enemies already opposed to it, for the object of gratuitous attack ? Does any rational person think that we should, under such circumstances, be in greater jeopardy than the Americans from these contentions?

Having already demonstrated that even Napoleon, with Europe at his feet, was powerless in his attacks upon our exports, we are afraid of being tedious in recurring to that subject.

Were a war once more to break forth over the Continent of Europe, and were we to stand aloof from the conflict, our commerce and manufactures, instead of receiving injury in any quarter, would be thereby benefited ; for, besides the well-known facilities which a state of warfare would give to the smuggler for supplying those very belligerents themselves with the products of our labour, it would, at the same time, put an end to the competition which we now sustain, in other parts of the world, from our manufacturing rivals of Europe. Germany, France, Switzerland, and Belgium, and, indeed, almost every nation of the Continent, for whose independence and existence we fought so long and arduously, have profited by the peace, to exclude our fabrics from their markets, and, in mistaken policy, borrowed from our own restrictive code, to raise up, at great sacrifices of national wealth, a manufacturing industry for themselves.

Thus we find that, at this moment, Prussia is completing a wall of tariffs, which she has been sedulously constructing for many years, and which will, more effectually than did Napoleon, exclude us from the German market—Prussia, for whom we bled, and for whose subsidies we are still taxed ! Austria, another of our costly allies, whose disasters our most renowned statesman* would not outlive—Austria has, ever since the peace, sealed her territory against our merchandise. Naples— that unworthy *protégé*, in behalf of whose court England's greatest hero † sullied his otherwise untarnished fame—Naples repays us with an impost of cent. per cent. upon our manufactures ; whilst France has, since Napoleon's fall, been a less profitable customer to England than she was during the time of his extremest enmity towards this country.

True, at the close of the war, our ministers might have

* Pitt.
† Nelson, Lady Hamilton, Prince Caraccioli.

stipulated for, and might have commanded a trade with all Europe, as some indemnity for our expenditure; but the warriors and statesmen who represented us at Vienna, and who took pains to forward such measures as the military occupation of France, or the erection of fortresses in Belgium, or the binding us to become guarantee for the permanency of the union of the Netherlands, forgot to utter one word about our merchants. It was unbecoming the dignity of our gallant and noble plenipotentiaries to stipulate for the welfare of the artisans and manufacturers of Great Britain. Compare this with the results of the cheap diplomacy of the Americans.

Alas! by what numberless arts, neglects, and caprices (to say nothing of crimes) have the interests of this industrious and greatly-favoured people been victimised!

Before closing this pamphlet, we will offer a few remarks as to the course which it behoves Great Britain to pursue, for the future, upon an important question of commercial policy.

With a view to enlarge, as much as possible, the capabilities of this people to support the burden of debt and taxation with which they are destined to be permanently loaded, every possible facility must be given to the increase of population, by the expansion of our foreign trade, and which can only be accomplished by repealing the protective duties on corn.

We shall be here met with the cry, that we are desirous of converting England into one vast manufactory, that we advocate the interests of our order, and so forth. Far from nourishing any such *esprit de corps*, our predilections lean altogether in an opposite direction. We were born and bred up amidst the pastoral charms of the south of England, and we confess to so much attachment to the pursuits of our forefathers (always provided that it be separated from the rick-burnings and pauperism of modern agriculture), that, had we the casting of the *rôle* of all the actors on this world's stage, we do not think we should suffer a cotton-mill or a manufactory to have a place in it; not that they remind us of "*billyrollers*," "*straps*," and "*infant martyrdoms*," for we never saw such; but we think a system which draws children from home, where they formerly worked in the company of parents, and under the wholesome restraint incident to disparity of years—nature's own moral safeguard of domestic life—to class them in factories, according to equality of age, to be productive of vice. But the factory system, which sprang from the discoveries in machinery, has been adopted in all the civilised nations of the world, and it is in vain for us to think of discountenancing its application to the necessities of this country; it only remains for us to mitigate, as far as possible, the evils that are, perhaps, not inseparably connected with this novel social element.

The present corn laws are founded on the principle of limiting, as far as possible, the growth of the population of Britain, within the means of the soil to supply it with subsistence. No candid advocate of a protective duty will deny that it must have this tendency; nor will he dispute that, to restrict the import of corn into a manufacturing nation, is to strike at the life of its foreign commerce.

It is objected by the landowners of England that, if the duty on grain were to be reduced, it would operate unfavourably upon their interests, and they claim a protection at the hands of the rest of society. Now, without entering at all into the question of the right which belongs to such pretensions, we shall content ourselves with taking our stand upon the simple ground of necessity, and declare that the people of this country are in an emergency that precludes the possibility of their ministering to the selfishness of any one class in the community.

The interest of the public debt cannot be paid except by the co-operation of our foreign commerce; and this cannot be preserved permanently, unless the price of that first element of the cost of our manufactures, *food*, be the same here as with our competitors abroad. We are surprised that the question has not before been placed in this point of view by the advocates of a free trade in corn, since it withdraws the subject altogether from that invidious position which it has hitherto held betwixt the rival contentions of agriculture and commerce, and places it under the control of inexorable State necessity.

We have been amazed (if anything could astonish us from this unintelligent party) to find that the national debt is one of the leading arguments made use of by the economists of the Sadler school, in advocating a restrictive duty on corn. A brief appeal to a very few simple facts will, we believe, not only deprive them of this argument, but, in the opinion of all unprejudiced minds, place it on the opposite side of the question.

Our public debt, funded and unfunded, amounts to about eight hundred millions. Let this sum be more fully appreciated, by bearing in mind that it exceeds the aggregate of all the debts of the whole world, including that of the East India Company, amounting to one hundred and fifty millions. Here, then, we have the British Empire, with only its twenty-five millions of population—possessing a territory of only ninety thousand square geographical miles, and containing only forty-five millions of acres of cultivated land (about two-thirds of the area of France), supporting an annual burden for the interest of the national debt, equal to the taxation borne, for the same purpose, by all other States. How, then, can a country, of so confined a boundary, and with no greater population than we have named, find it possible to endure so great a disproportion of taxation ? If it be asked, how does France meet her public expenses, we can answer, by pointing to the superabundant production of wine, oil, silk, tobacco, fruit, and corn, yielded throughout an expanse of territory so wide as to ensure an almost perpetual harvest to its people. If we inquire, how does Russia maintain her government burdens—the surplus timber, corn, hemp, and tallow of that country must be the reply. Would we know by what resources Italy, Spain, and America discharge their respective national encumbrances —the excess of the produce of silk, oil, fruits, cotton, and tobacco, over and above the wants of the population of those countries, solves the mystery.

But we demand to know by what means Great Britain can sustain an annual burden, for interest of debt, exceeding that of these and all other States together. Is it out of the surplus production of its corn? Her soil has not, for the last forty years, yielded sufficient to supply the necessities of her population. Is this enormous demand satisfied by the yearly excess of her wines, silk, oil, fruits, cotton, or tobacco? The sterile land and inhospitable climate of Britain are incapable of producing any one of these. Where, then, lies the secret of her wealth? Is it in her colonies? How, if we are prepared to prove that these are at this moment, and, in future, are still more destined to become, a severe burden to the people of these realms?

Our mineral riches are the means by which alone we have been enabled to incur this debt, and by whose agency only can we at this moment discharge the interest of it.

To satisfy ourselves of this, let us examine the year's return of our revenue, and we shall there discover nearly twenty millions of income under the head of customs duties. How are the commodities, on which this amount of taxation is levied, obtained from foreigners? Are they received in exchange for our agricultural produce? By looking over the list of articles exported, we shall, on the contrary, find that out of thirty-six millions of home products not one million is the unmixed growth of the soil.

These commodities are purchased by our cottons, woollens,* hardware, and the other articles produced by the manufacturers of this country; the growth, to use the term, of the coal and

* We have the testimony of the Leeds manufacturers, in their evidence before the legislature, that foreign wools are absolutely indispensable to our Yorkshire industry.

iron of Great Britain—which are, we repeat, the primary sources of all her wealth and power, and the want of which alone prevents other nations of Europe from rivalling her in manufacturing greatness. Of course it is known that our agricultural labour supplies a great portion of the food of our weavers and other artizans, and, therefore, mixes with the results of their industry ; but when it is recollected that the cost of food here is from fifty to one hundred and fifty per cent. dearer than in other States, it will be admitted that it is not owing to the cheap price at which the farmer supplies the corn of the manufacturer that the latter is enabled to undersell his foreign competitors.

To come to the point with those who advocate a restrictive policy on our foreign trade, by a protection, as it is called, of our agriculture, we ask, in what way do they propose ever to pay off the national debt, or permanently to discharge the interest of it, out of the indigenous wealth of these islands ?

The whole area of cultivated land in this monarchy is, as we have before stated, estimated at about forty-five millions of acres : at twenty pounds per acre, the fee simple of the soil of these islands (we, of course, leave out the houses, &c.) would very little exceed the amount of our debt. There is an end, therefore, of the idea of discharging the principal out of the real property of the country ; and by what means would they who obstruct a foreign commerce profess to pay the interest of the debt without the assistance of that trade ? Supposing that our exports were diminished, and that, owing to the consequent falling off in our imports, our customs were sensibly reduced, from what articles of our agricultural produce would these advocates of a Japanese policy raise the deficient revenue ? In France (where the prohibitive system, which has long reigned supremely, is drawing fast to a dismal end) the customs duties amount to about one-fifth of our own, and the great bulk of the revenue is levied from the land. But provided that a reduction of our foreign trade rendered such a step necessary, we ask again and it is an important question, involving the whole gist of our argument), upon what branch of British agriculture could an augmented impost be levied ? May not the recent almost fanatical outcry against the malt tax, the only burden of any magnitude borne directly by the land in this country, serve as a sufficient answer to the inquiry ?

The question of the repeal of the corn laws, then, re-solves itself into one of absolute state necessity ; since our foreign trade, which is indispensable to the payment of the interest of the national debt, cannot be permanently preserved if we persevere in a restrictive duty against the principal article of exchange of rude, unmanufacturing people. To prohibit the import of corn, such as is actually the case at this moment, is to strangle infant commerce in its cradle ; nay, worse, it is to destroy it even in its mother's womb.

We recommend the landowners, but especially the great proprietors who constitute the upper house of legislature, to reflect upon this view of the corn laws.

But we have remarked an inclination in a part of the landed interest to slight—to use the mildest possible term—the public creditor ; a feeling that shone forth in the motion of the Marquis of Chandos to remove the malt tax—thus aiming at the insolvency of the Chancellor of the Exchequer—without caring first to inquire by what fresh imposts he should meet the engagements of his country. These unreflecting minds are, we apprehend, quite incapable of estimating the consequences that will ensue if ever we should be found unable to meet the interest of the debt—in other words, if the British nation should be declared bankrupt ! Let us for one moment contemplate the results that would follow from such an event.

We find, from a statement in " Porter's Official Tables," that there are 250,000 persons receiving dividends, of and under the amount of £200 a year. Presuming the families or dependents of them to average * two each, then we shall have here half a million of individuals looking to the public funds for support. Moreover, we find the total amount of the deposits in all the savings' banks of the kingdom to be £13,500,000 ; and the number of depositors, according to the same authority, is 412,217, averaging £33 each ; taking the families or dependents of these at the same average as before, and it gives three-quarters of a million more. Then there is an immense amount of the public debt owing to charities,—including insurance offices, benefit clubs, schools, &c., involving the interests of an incalculable multitude of necessitous persons. Guessing these to amount to only the same total as the last mentioned (for it is impossible to form a correct estimate on the subject), then we arrive at an aggregate of two millions of the middle and lower classes, who are, directly or indirectly, claimants on the national debt.

Now, no one capable of thinking upon such a subject at all will for a moment believe that, if we were driven to such an extremity as to rob these two millions—comprising so many of the labourers, the small traders, the orphans and widows —of their subsistence, that the pomp of the court or the wealth of the clergy, or the privileges of our nobles, would be more secure than the bread of these humble annuitants.

No rational mind can suppose that lords in waiting, grooms of the stole, gold sticks and silver sticks, would be maintained —that bishops and prebends would still be found in undisturbed possession of their stalls and revenues—or that the peers would retain their law of primogeniture, or the right of hereditary legislation, whilst desolation and misery overspread the land with horrors as terrible as any it could undergo from the ravages of half-a-million of Cossacks.†

* To avoid exaggeration, we have named a lower average than we are entitled to quote.

† Here let us remark, in reference to the absurdest of all absurd chimeras with which we haun ourselves, of this empire being in danger from the assaults

The cleverest of our journalists has said—and the words have passed into a proverb—"Before you rob the public creditor, send your throne to the pawn-shop." And nothing can be more certain than that the national debt (which ought never to have been incurred, and the authors of which some future generation will probably deem to have been madmen) must be borne by the people of England, entire and untouched, so long as they can stand beneath its burden. If ever the day should come that sees this mighty fabric crush the nation to the dust, it will bury in its ruins the monarchy, Church, and aristocracy, with every vestige of our feudal institutions, and every ancestral precedent—leaving the state, like Mr. Courtenay's sheet of blank paper, upon which the then existing generation will have the task of inscribing a new constitution, borrowed from the freest and most flourishing community of that day, and which, in all probability, will be found on the continent of America.

From such a catastrophe there is no escape but in either honestly paying off the principal of the public debt, or in continuing to discharge the interest of it for ever. The ravings after an equitable adjustment, and other like expedients, are but the impracticable schemes of those who would wish to precipitate such a calamity as we have been describing.

If every house in England were converted into a Court of Chancery, and if all the men between twenty and sixty were constituted Lord Chancellors, there would not then be a sufficient quantity of equity courts and equity judges to effect such an equitable adjustment of the national debt as is meant, during the life-time of an entire generation.

The national debt, then, is inviolable; and this recalls us to the inquiry of how it is to be permanently supported; which brings us again to the question of the corn laws.

of Russia—that we are convinced there is, at this moment, ten thousand times more cause of apprehension from the financial evils of Great Britain than from all the powers of the world.

The only way in which we can lighten the pressure of the debt is by adding to the population and wealth of the country. The agricultural districts have, we suspect – so far as the middle classes are concerned — already experienced that dull state incident to the stationary period of society; whilst, under the present amended poor laws, we believe that the farther increase of the pauper population will be effectually checked. The sole way, then, of adding to our numbers, is to give the freest possible development to the only present superabundant contents of the soil—the mineral products of Great Britain.

By repealing the present corn laws, and putting only a fixed duty of such an amount as would bring the greatest revenue (we object no more to a tax on corn than on tea or sugar, for the purpose of revenue,* but we oppose a *protective* duty, as it is called), which, probably, might be found to be two shillings a quarter, such an impulse would be given to the manufactures of this country, whilst so great a shock would be experienced by our rivals, from the augmented price of food all over the world, that a rapid growth of wealth and increase of numbers must take place throughout the coal and iron districts of England, Wales, and Scotland.

The population of Staffordshire, Lancashire, Yorkshire, Lanarkshire, and of counties adjacent to these, might be trebled in the course of a couple of generations ; and there would be no limit to its increase but in the contents of our coal mines, to which geologists assign a duration varying from two to three thousand years !

It will be asked, what would be the effects of such a change upon the agriculture of the country ?   The best way of replying to this question is to consider what must have been the consequence to all interests in this country if, in lieu of the restrictions put upon the import of corn in 1816, a law had been passed, imposing only such a moderate duty as would

* [Mr. Cobden soon afterwards acknowledged his error.   *See* Prentice's History of the League, vol. i., p. 194.]

ultimately produce the greatest revenue, and which, in our opinion, would be found to be two shillings a quarter. The factory system would in all probability not have taken place in America or Germany;—it most certainly could not have flourished, as it has done, both in those states, and in France, Belgium, and Switzerland, through the fostering bounties which the high-priced food of the British artisan has offered to the cheaper fed manufacturer of those countries.

Our belief, after some reflection upon this question, is (having already very far exceeded the intended limits of this pamphlet, we are precluded from going into details), that, had a wise modification of our corn laws been effected at the close of the war, the official value of our exports would have exceeded by one-third its present amount. This is, of course, presuming that our manufacturing population had augmented proportionately ;—we believe that, under such circumstances, the beforementioned counties would have now sustained upwards of a million more than their present numbers ; but, as the increase of their inhabitants would not have been equal to the demand for labour, a great immigration must have taken place from the agricultural districts. This would have saved those quarters that frightful ordeal of pauperism and crime with which they have disgraced our modern history. The farmer would, by the offer of other resources for his family and dependents, have been saved from the state of servility into which he is plunged. Instead of the rent of the tenants being dictated by the landlords, the former would, under this more favourable state of things, have been the arbiters of the incomes of the latter. In short, the buyers—*i.e.*, the farmers—would, in this case, as the purchasers do in dealing with all other commodities, have decided the prices of their farms—they would not have been, as at present, determined by the sellers, *i.e.*, the landowners.

Under such an assumed state of things, this country would, we believe, by this time have acquired an increase to its present wealth to the extent of 350* millions—nearly one-half the amount of the national debt.

The immediate effects of all this to the landed proprietor would clearly have been a reduction of rent; or where the property was heavily encumbered, his estates would have passed into other hands.

We should not, in such a case, have heard of those displays of wanton extravagance that tend so much to demoralise all classes. Instead of the exhibitions of prodigality and insolence abroad, with which some of those proprietors affronted the nations of the continent, and disgraced at the same time their native country—instead of their contributing at home to raise and support a palace for Crockford—instead of their dispensing with all decorum, and herding with grooms and black-legs at Newmarket or Doncaster—instead of the necessary consequences of all this, the subsequent ruin and exile of such wastrels†—in place of these things, we might have beheld a provident and virtuous proprietary residing principally upon and managing their estates; and who, we verily believe, would, under this supposed state of things, have become richer in wealth, as well as honour, than they are at this day.

But selfishness, which is ever short-sighted, has hitherto governed supremely the destinies of this empire ; and we have seen how disastrous has been its rule, not only to its own interests, but to the prosperity of the nation at large. Should the same misgovernment from no better motives be persevered in with respect to the corn question, the effects will be still more calamitous for the future. The public debt, "that eternal ally of truth and justice" (to use the words of a famous political writer, without adopting his malignancy), will visit with terrible reprisals the monopolists who shall persist in upholding the present corn laws.

---

* It is estimated that our annual loss on corn alone is nine millions.

† *Wastrel*, in Lancashire phrase, an idle, debauched, and worthless spend-thrift—a word that may be useful in London.

We cannot do better than conclude with the words of an intelligent American, as they were addressed to an English traveller. The extract is taken from the preface to " Ferguson's Tour in Canada and a portion of the United States."

" Even with your present burden of debt, if your Government were to renounce all interference with the affairs of the continent, and keep no more force, land or naval, than is necessary for your own security, have no more wars, and diminish the expenditure as much as possible, you will grow so rapidly in the next fifty years that your debt would cease to be of any importance. I earnestly hope that the passage of the Reform Bill may be only the prelude to an entire change of system ; and that your successors may feel, as we do here, that wars do not promote the prosperity of a nation, and have the good sense to avoid them."

1 2 3 4 5 6 7 8 9 10 11 12 13   88 87 86 85 84 83 82 81 80